The Vintage Christmas Revival Guide

Nostalgic Crafts, Retro Recipes, and Timeless Traditions to Recreate a Classic Holiday at Home

James Holloway

Contents

1. Introduction: The Magic of a Nostalgic Christmas   1

    PART I
    Recipes: Classic Christmas Comfort Food   5

    PART II
    Crafts: Handmade Christmas Decorations   47

    PART III
    Decor: Transforming Your Home into a Cozy Christmas Haven   73

2. Holiday Traditions to Bring Back   94
3. Wrapping & Gifting: The Art of Handmade Presents   102
4. Playlist & Media Recommendation   110
5. Final Touches: Hosting a Nostalgic Christmas Party   119
6. Resource Section   127

    Afterword: The Timeless Magic of Christmas   137

Introduction: The Magic of a Nostalgic Christmas

There's something about Christmas that tugs at the heartstrings like no other time of year. It's a season wrapped in warmth, memories, and tradition. Whether it's the smell of freshly baked cookies filling the house, the twinkling lights adorning the tree, or the simple joy of giving and receiving handmade gifts, Christmas evokes a sense of nostalgia that brings us back to simpler, more meaningful moments. This book is an invitation to step back in time, slow down, and rediscover the charm of Christmases past.

In today's fast-paced, technology-driven world, it's easy to lose touch with the rituals that once made this season so special. The handmade crafts, the comforting recipes passed down from generation to generation, the decorations lovingly made from everyday materials—these elements of Christmas were more than just traditions. They were moments to connect with family, friends, and the deeper spirit of the season. They reflected a time when every decoration, dish, and gift carried a story, woven with care and thoughtfulness.

This guidebook is designed to help you recreate that sense of nostalgia—a Christmas full of warmth, creativity, and old-fashioned joy.

Whether you're longing for the Victorian elegance of candlelit trees and spiced plum puddings, the mid-century sparkle of tinsel and aluminium trees, or the rustic simplicity of homemade crafts and cozy gatherings, you'll find inspiration here to bring the magic of the past into your home today.

Inside these pages, you'll discover time-honoured recipes that have graced holiday tables for decades, from the rich, spiced flavours of traditional fruitcake to the delightful crunch of gingerbread cookies. You'll learn how to craft handmade decorations that evoke the charm of simpler times, from the natural beauty of evergreen wreaths to glittering ornaments made with love. And you'll find ideas for creating a holiday atmosphere that feels both timeless and intimate—whether that's with vintage-inspired decor, classic Christmas music, or holiday traditions long forgotten.

This is more than just a collection of recipes and crafts; it's an experience, a chance to slow down and savour the moments that make Christmas truly magical.

So, pour yourself a cup of hot cocoa, turn on the Christmas lights, and let's journey back to the heart of Christmas, where joy is found in the simple things—good food, thoughtful gifts, and the company of loved ones. Together, we'll bring the nostalgia of yesteryear into the present, creating a holiday season filled with warmth, wonder, and memories to last a lifetime.

Welcome to your nostalgic Christmas.

Let the magic begin.

Part One
Recipes: Classic Christmas Comfort Food

There's a certain kind of magic that comes from the kitchen during the holidays—a magic woven through the comforting aromas of spices, butter, and sugar, and the familiar sounds of family bustling around the oven.

In this chapter, we're bringing back the heartwarming, timeless recipes that have been at the centre of Christmas celebrations for generations.

These dishes don't just satisfy hunger; they tell stories, evoke memories, and bring people together around the table, just as they did decades ago.

From Victorian elegance to mid-century favourites, these classic recipes are all about comfort, nostalgia, and tradition.

Whether you're looking to recreate the rich, spiced flavorus of an old-fashioned fruitcake or the simple joy of baking cookies with loved ones, the recipes in this chapter will help you capture the essence of a Christmas from the past.

Victorian Christmas Recipes

The Victorians are often credited with creating many of the Christmas traditions we know and love today, and their holiday feasts were nothing short of spectacular. During this era, Christmas meals were lavish, yet each dish was made with simple, wholesome ingredients. The recipes below will take you back to a time when plum pudding steamed for hours, the smell of roasted chestnuts filled the air, and tables were set with opulent displays of fruits and spices.

PLUM PUDDING (TRADITIONAL WITH A MODERN TWIST)

Plum pudding is one of the most iconic Victorian Christmas desserts, traditionally made weeks in advance and steamed for hours. It was often wrapped in cloth, boiled, and filled with spices, dried fruits, and suet. Here's a step-by-step guide for making a traditional version with a modern variation to make it easier and more accessible.

Ingredients (Traditional Version):

- 250g suet (beef or vegetable) or butter (for modern variation)
- 150g brown sugar
- 150g fresh breadcrumbs
- 150g all-purpose flour
- 1 tsp ground cinnamon
- 1 tsp ground nutmeg
- 1 tsp ground cloves
- 1/2 tsp ground ginger
- 300g mixed dried fruit (raisins, currants, and sultanas)
- 100g candied peel (optional)
- 1 grated apple
- Zest of 1 lemon and 1 orange
- 2 tbsp black treacle (or molasses)
- 3 large eggs
- 100ml dark rum, brandy, or stout
- Pinch of salt

INSTRUCTIONS:

1. **Prepare the Batter:** In a large mixing bowl, combine the suet (or butter), sugar, breadcrumbs, and flour. Stir in the spices, dried fruit, candied peel (if using), grated apple, and citrus zest.
2. **Add Wet Ingredients:** Stir in the treacle, eggs, and rum/brandy/stout. Mix until fully combined, and the batter has a sticky consistency.
3. **Steaming the Pudding:** Grease a pudding basin or a heatproof bowl. Spoon the mixture into the basin, leaving some room at the top for expansion. Cover with a piece of parchment paper and aluminium foil, tying it securely with string.
4. **Steam:** Place the basin in a large pot with a trivet or upturned saucer at the bottom (so the pudding doesn't touch the bottom of the pot). Fill the pot halfway with boiling water. Cover and steam for 6 hours, checking occasionally to top up with water.
5. **Cool and Store:** Once cooked, remove the pudding and let it cool. Store it in a cool, dry place. Traditionally, plum pudding is made weeks before Christmas to allow the flavours to mature.
6. **Serve:** To serve, reheat the pudding by steaming for another 2 hours. For a dramatic touch, pour a little brandy over the top and set it alight just before serving!

MODERN VARIATION:

For a quicker version, use butter instead of suet, and replace steaming with baking:

- After step 2, spoon the mixture into greased muffin tins for individual servings and bake at 180°C (350°F) for 30-40 minutes, or until firm to the touch. This cuts down the preparation time while still offering a rich, flavourful dessert.

MINCE PIES

MINCE PIES HAVE BEEN a beloved part of British Christmas since the Middle Ages, though their filling has evolved. In the Victorian era, mince pies contained a mixture of dried fruits, suet, and spices, but no longer included meat. Here's a recipe for homemade mince pies with a delightful filling made from scratch.

INGREDIENTS (MAKES 12):
For the Pastry:

- 225g plain flour
- 125g cold butter, cubed
- 2 tbsp icing sugar (optional for a sweeter crust)
- 1 egg yolk
- Cold water (as needed)

For the Mince Filling:

- 200g raisins
- 100g currants
- 100g sultanas
- 50g candied peel
- 1 apple, peeled and finely chopped
- Zest and juice of 1 orange
- 75g brown sugar
- 50g suet (or butter for a vegetarian option)
- 1 tsp ground cinnamon
- 1/2 tsp ground nutmeg
- 1/4 tsp ground cloves
- 50ml brandy or rum

Instructions:

1. **Prepare the Mince Filling:**
   - Combine all the ingredients for the filling in a large bowl. Stir well to coat the fruit and spices with the brandy. Cover and leave to sit overnight or for at least a few hours to let the flavours meld.
2. **Make the Pastry:**
   - Sift the flour into a bowl, add the cold butter cubes, and rub together with your fingertips until the mixture resembles breadcrumbs. Stir in the icing sugar if using.
   - Add the egg yolk and a little cold water (1 tbsp at a time) to bring the dough together. Wrap in cling film and refrigerate for 30 minutes.
3. **Assemble the Pies:**
   - Preheat your oven to 180°C (350°F). Roll out the pastry on a floured surface to about 3mm thick. Use a round cutter (about 8-9cm) to cut circles for the pie bases and a slightly smaller cutter for the lids.
   - Press the larger circles into a 12-hole muffin tin. Spoon the mince filling into each, being careful not to overfill. Top with the smaller pastry rounds, pressing the edges together lightly.
4. **Bake:**
   - Brush the tops with a little beaten egg and make a small slit in the top of each pie. Bake for 20-25 minutes, until the pastry is golden and crisp.
5. **Serve:**
   - Let the mince pies cool slightly before removing from the tin. Dust with powdered sugar and serve warm or at room temperature.

The Vintage Christmas Revival Guide

Mince pies have been a beloved part of British Christmas since the Middle Ages

ROASTED CHESTNUTS

Roasted chestnuts were a favourite street food in Victorian England and a symbol of cozy Christmas gatherings. The tradition of roasting chestnuts over an open fire evokes warmth and the joy of the season. Here's how to prepare them at home, whether you have a fireplace or just an oven.

INGREDIENTS:

- Fresh chestnuts (as many as you like)
- A pinch of salt (optional)
- Butter (optional, for serving)

Instructions:

1. **Score the Chestnuts:**
   - Using a sharp knife, carefully cut an "X" on the flat side of each chestnut. This helps release steam and makes them easier to peel after roasting.
2. **Roast Over the Fire:**
   - If you have access to an open fire, place the chestnuts in a roasting pan or a perforated chestnut roaster and hold them over the flames. Shake the pan occasionally to cook evenly. Roast for 15-20 minutes, or until the shells start to peel back and the nuts are tender.
3. **Roasting in the Oven:**
   - Preheat the oven to 200°C (400°F). Place the scored chestnuts on a baking sheet in a single layer. Roast for 20-25 minutes, or until the shells start to open and the chestnuts are soft inside.

Check on them halfway through and turn them for even cooking.

4. **Serve:**
    - Once roasted, wrap the chestnuts in a kitchen towel to keep warm and let them rest for about 10 minutes. This will make them easier to peel. Serve warm, with a sprinkle of salt or a dab of butter for extra richness if desired.

Tips:

- Roasted chestnuts are best eaten fresh while still warm. They have a sweet, nutty flavour and a soft texture that complements many Christmas meals or can be enjoyed on their own.
- For a holiday twist, serve the roasted chestnuts alongside a glass of mulled wine or cider for a traditional pairing.

THESE VICTORIAN RECIPES not only capture the nostalgic flavours of Christmas past but also offer modern adaptations that bring them to life in today's kitchens. Whether you're steaming a rich plum pudding, baking mince pies from scratch, or roasting chestnuts by the fire, each of these recipes will evoke the warmth and coziness of a traditional Victorian Christmas.

1940s & 1950s Christmas Dishes

The 1940s and 1950s were marked by festive family gatherings and classic, hearty Christmas dishes. During this time, the holiday table often featured traditional meats like ham or turkey, quirky sides like Jell-O molouds or ambrosia salad, and a fruitcake that was passed down through generations. These recipes combine the retro charm of the era with modern tweaks to fit today's tastes.

HONEY BAKED HAM OR ROAST TURKEY

Both **honey-baked ham** and **roast turkey** were mainstays on Christmas tables in the mid-20th century. While turkey was often associated with Thanksgiving, it also made appearances at Christmas dinners, especially in larger family gatherings. Ham, with its sweet glaze and savoury meat, became a popular choice in the 1950s for a simpler but flavourful centrepiece.

Honey-Baked Ham Recipe
Ingredients:

- 1 bone-in smoked ham (about 5-6kg)
- 1/2 cup honey
- 1/2 cup brown sugar
- 2 tbsp Dijon mustard
- 1 tbsp apple cider vinegar
- 1 tsp ground cloves
- 1/2 tsp ground cinnamon
- 1/4 tsp ground ginger

Instructions:

1. **Prepare the Ham:**
   - Preheat your oven to 160°C (325°F). Place the ham, cut side down, on a rack in a large roasting pan. Score the surface of the ham in a diamond pattern, making shallow cuts with a sharp knife.
2. **Make the Glaze:**
   - In a small saucepan, combine honey, brown sugar, Dijon mustard, apple cider vinegar, ground cloves,

cinnamon, and ginger. Stir over medium heat until the sugar dissolves and the glaze thickens slightly.

3. **Bake the Ham:**
    - Brush a layer of the glaze over the ham and cover it loosely with foil. Bake for about 1 1/2 to 2 hours (roughly 20 minutes per pound), basting every 20-30 minutes with more glaze.
    - For the final 30 minutes, remove the foil and let the glaze caramelise, giving the ham a rich, golden-brown finish.

4. **Serve:**
    - Let the ham rest for 10 minutes before slicing. Serve warm, with any extra glaze drizzled over the slices.

Roast Turkey with Vintage Gravy Recipe
Ingredients for the Turkey:

- 1 whole turkey (4-5kg)
- 100g butter, softened
- Salt and pepper
- 2 onions, quartered
- 2 lemons, halved
- 2 sprigs of fresh rosemary
- 1 cup chicken or turkey broth (for basting)

Instructions:

1. **Prepare the Turkey:**
    - Preheat the oven to 180°C (350°F). Rinse the turkey inside and out and pat dry with paper towels. Rub the turkey generously with softened butter, then season all over with salt and pepper.

- Stuff the cavity with the quartered onions, lemons, and rosemary.
2. **Roast:**
    - Place the turkey in a large roasting pan. Cover the turkey loosely with foil and roast for about 3-4 hours (roughly 15 minutes per pound), basting every 30 minutes with broth and pan juices.
    - For the last 45 minutes, remove the foil to allow the skin to brown and crisp.
3. **Rest and Carve:**
    - Once the turkey reaches an internal temperature of 75°C (165°F), remove it from the oven and let it rest for 20-30 minutes before carving.

Vintage Gravy Recipe
Ingredients:

- Turkey drippings (from the roasting pan)
- 1/4 cup all-purpose flour
- 2 cups turkey or chicken broth
- Salt and pepper to taste

Instructions:

1. **Make the Gravy:**
    - After roasting the turkey, carefully pour the drippings from the pan into a heatproof bowl and let it sit for a few minutes. Skim off any excess fat from the top.
    - Place the roasting pan on the stovetop over medium heat and add the flour, stirring to form a roux. Slowly whisk in the reserved drippings and

broth, stirring constantly until smooth and thickened.
- Season with salt and pepper to taste, and simmer for a few minutes to blend the flavours.

AMBROSIA SALAD OR JELL-O-MOULD

Both **ambrosia salad** and **Jell-O moulds** became iconic in the mid-century American kitchen, celebrated for their quirky charm and vibrant presentation. Ambrosia salad was a popular Southern dessert, often made with canned fruits and sweetened coconut, while Jell-O moulds became a symbol of innovation in convenience cooking.

Ambrosia Salad Recipe (Retro with a Modern Twist)
Ingredients:

- 1 cup mandarin oranges (canned or fresh)
- 1 cup pineapple chunks (canned or fresh)
- 1 cup shredded sweetened coconut
- 1 cup mini marshmallows
- 1 cup sour cream or whipped cream (for a lighter version, use Greek yogurt)
- 1/2 cup maraschino cherries (optional)
- 1/4 cup chopped pecans (optional)

Instructions:

1. **Mix the Ingredients:**
    - In a large mixing bowl, combine the mandarin oranges, pineapple chunks, coconut, marshmallows, and maraschino cherries (if using).
2. **Fold in the Cream:**
    - Gently fold in the sour cream or whipped cream until everything is evenly coated. For a lighter

twist, you can substitute sour cream with Greek yogurt.
3. **Chill and Serve:**
   - Refrigerate the ambrosia salad for at least an hour before serving, allowing the flavors to meld. Sprinkle chopped pecans on top before serving if desired.

Retro Jell-O Mold Recipe
Ingredients:

- 1 box (85g) flavoured gelatin (lime, raspberry, or orange are classic choices)
- 1 1/2 cups boiling water
- 1/2 cup cold water
- 1/2 cup crushed pineapple (drained)
- 1/2 cup cottage cheese (for a vintage touch)
- 1/2 cup whipped cream or Cool Whip

Instructions:

1. **Dissolve the Gelatin:**
   - In a large bowl, dissolve the flavoured gelatin in 1 1/2 cups boiling water. Stir until completely dissolved.
2. **Add Cold Water and Ingredients:**
   - Stir in the cold water, then gently fold in the crushed pineapple and cottage cheese.
3. **Set the Mould:**
   - Pour the mixture into a Jell-O mould or bundt pan. Refrigerate for 4-6 hours, or until fully set.

The Vintage Christmas Revival Guide

4. **Unmould and Serve:**
   - To unmould, dip the mould briefly in warm water, then invert it onto a serving plate. Top with a dollop of whipped cream or Cool Whip before serving.

During the 1940's Jell-O mold's became a symbol of innovation in convenience cooking

RETRO FRUITCAKE

FRUITCAKE OFTEN GETS A BAD REPUTATION, but with the right approach, this **retro fruitcake** can be a delicious addition to your Christmas table. Using homemade candied fruits and a balanced blend of spices, this recipe makes a moist and flavourful cake that's far from the dense, overly sweetened versions of the past.

Ingredients for Homemade Candied Fruits:

- 1 cup dried apricots, chopped
- 1 cup dried figs, chopped
- 1 cup dried cherries or cranberries
- 1/2 cup candied citrus peel
- 1/2 cup raisins or currants
- 1/4 cup rum or brandy (optional, for soaking)

Ingredients for the Fruitcake:

- 225g unsalted butter, softened
- 200g brown sugar
- 3 large eggs
- 250g all-purpose flour
- 1/2 tsp ground cinnamon
- 1/2 tsp ground nutmeg
- 1/4 tsp ground cloves
- 1/4 tsp salt
- Zest of 1 orange
- Zest of 1 lemon
- 1/2 cup chopped nuts (walnuts or pecans)
- 1/4 cup brandy or rum (optional, for brushing)

Instructions:

1. **Prepare the Candied Fruit:**
   - Combine the dried fruits and candied peel in a bowl. If using, soak them in the rum or brandy for several hours or overnight.
2. **Make the Batter:**
   - Preheat the oven to 150°C (300°F). Cream together the butter and brown sugar until light and fluffy. Add the eggs one at a time, beating well after each addition.
3. **Add Dry Ingredients:**
   - In a separate bowl, whisk together the flour, cinnamon, nutmeg, cloves, and salt. Gradually add the flour mixture to the butter mixture, stirring until just combined. Stir in the orange and lemon zests, soaked fruit (with or without the liquid), and chopped nuts.
4. **Bake:**
   - Grease and line a loaf pan or cake tin. Pour the batter into the prepared pan, smoothing the top. Bake for 1 1/2 to 2 hours, or until a skewer inserted into the centre comes out clean.

1. **Cool and Brush with Brandy:**
   - Allow the fruitcake to cool in the pan for 15 minutes, then turn out onto a wire rack to cool completely. For added moisture and flavour, brush the top and sides of the cake with a little brandy or rum while it's still warm. You can repeat this process a few times over the next few days to enhance the flavour and keep the cake moist.

1. **Store and Serve:**
    - Wrap the fruitcake in parchment paper and foil, and store in an airtight container. Fruitcakes can be made weeks ahead, as their flavours deepen over time. When ready to serve, slice and enjoy with tea or coffee for a nostalgic holiday treat.

1960s & 1970s Christmas Cookies

During the 1960s and 1970s, Christmas cookies became a cherished holiday tradition, with families baking together to create beautifully decorated treats. Iconic cookies like **gingerbread men** and **sugar cookies** were often decorated with colourful icing and sprinkles, while **rum balls** and **snowball cookies** added a festive touch to the holiday cookie tray. These classic recipes capture the charm and warmth of the era, bringing back memories of homemade holiday sweets enjoyed around the tree.

GINGERBREAD MEN COOKIES

GINGERBREAD MEN ARE a quintessential Christmas treat, their spiced flavour and whimsical shapes bringing a sense of nostalgia to any holiday gathering. This classic recipe is perfect for cutting into festive shapes and decorating with icing and candies.

INGREDIENTS:

- 350g all-purpose flour
- 1 tsp baking soda
- 2 tsp ground ginger
- 1 tsp ground cinnamon
- 1/2 tsp ground cloves
- 1/2 tsp ground nutmeg
- 1/4 tsp salt
- 150g unsalted butter, softened
- 100g brown sugar
- 1 large egg
- 4 tbsp molasses or dark treacle
- 2 tsp vanilla extract

Instructions:

1. **Make the Dough:**
    - In a medium bowl, sift together the flour, baking soda, ginger, cinnamon, cloves, nutmeg, and salt.
    - In a separate large bowl, cream the butter and brown sugar together until light and fluffy. Add the egg, molasses, and vanilla, and beat until well combined.

- Gradually add the dry ingredients to the wet mixture, mixing until the dough forms. Divide the dough into two portions, wrap in plastic wrap, and chill in the refrigerator for at least 2 hours.

2. **Roll and Cut:**
    - Preheat the oven to 180°C (350°F). Roll out the chilled dough on a lightly floured surface to about 5mm (1/4 inch) thickness. Use gingerbread man cookie cutters (or other festive shapes) to cut out the cookies.
    - Place the cookies on a parchment-lined baking sheet, leaving space between them.

3. **Bake:**
    - Bake for 10-12 minutes, or until the edges are lightly browned. Let the cookies cool on the baking sheet for a few minutes before transferring to a wire rack to cool completely.

4. **Decorate:**
    - Once the cookies have cooled, decorate using royal icing and small candies like chocolate chips or sprinkles. You can pipe the icing to create the traditional gingerbread man look, adding buttons, smiles, and eyes.

SUGAR COOKIES

Sugar cookies are a timeless classic, especially during the holiday season. With a crisp, buttery texture and a sweet vanilla flavour, these cookies are perfect for cutting into festive shapes and decorating with icing, sprinkles, or edible glitter.

Ingredients:

- 300g all-purpose flour
- 1/2 tsp baking powder
- 1/4 tsp salt
- 225g unsalted butter, softened
- 200g granulated sugar
- 1 large egg
- 2 tsp vanilla extract

Instructions:

1. **Make the Dough:**
    - In a medium bowl, whisk together the flour, baking powder, and salt.
    - In a large bowl, cream the butter and sugar together until light and fluffy. Beat in the egg and vanilla extract until combined.
    - Gradually add the dry ingredients to the wet ingredients, mixing until a smooth dough forms. Divide the dough in half, wrap each portion in plastic wrap, and refrigerate for at least 1 hour.
2. **Roll and Cut:**
    - Preheat the oven to 180°C (350°F). Roll out the dough on a floured surface to about 5mm (1/4

inch) thickness. Use holiday-themed cookie cutters (stars, trees, bells) to cut out the cookies.
- Transfer the cookies to a parchment-lined baking sheet.

3. **Bake:**
   - Bake for 8-10 minutes, or until the edges are lightly golden. Let the cookies cool on the baking sheet for a few minutes before transferring to a wire rack to cool completely.

4. **Decorate:**
   - Decorate the cooled cookies with royal icing, sprinkles, edible glitter, or coloured sugar. For a nostalgic touch, use a piping bag to create classic holiday designs, like snowflakes or stars.

RUM BALLS

Rum balls are a no-bake treat that became incredibly popular in the 1960s. These rich, chocolatey bites are flavoured with dark rum and rolled in powdered sugar, making them a festive indulgence. They're perfect for holiday cookie platters or as an edible gift.

Ingredients:

- 200g crushed vanilla wafers or digestive biscuits
- 100g powdered sugar (plus extra for rolling)
- 2 tbsp cocoa powder
- 1/2 cup dark rum
- 1 tsp vanilla extract
- 100g finely chopped nuts (walnuts or pecans)
- 2 tbsp light corn syrup or honey

Instructions:

1. **Make the Mixture:**
    - In a large bowl, combine the crushed wafers or biscuits, powdered sugar, cocoa powder, and chopped nuts.
    - Stir in the rum, vanilla extract, and corn syrup (or honey). Mix until the ingredients come together to form a thick, sticky dough.
2. **Form the Balls:**
    - Roll the mixture into small, bite-sized balls (about 1 inch in diameter).
3. **Coat and Chill:**
    - Roll each ball in powdered sugar until fully coated. Place the rum balls on a baking sheet lined

with parchment paper and refrigerate for at least 2 hours before serving. Store in an airtight container for up to a week, allowing the flavours to intensify over time.

SNOWBALL COOKIES

Snowball cookies (also known as **Russian tea cakes** or **Mexican wedding cookies**) are light, buttery, nutty cookies rolled in powdered sugar, giving them their signature "snowball" appearance. They melt in your mouth and add a lovely, nostalgic charm to holiday cookie trays.

Ingredients:

- 225g unsalted butter, softened
- 100g powdered sugar (plus extra for rolling)
- 1 tsp vanilla extract
- 300g all-purpose flour
- 1/4 tsp salt
- 100g finely chopped pecans or walnuts

Instructions:

1. **Make the Dough:**
   - In a large bowl, beat the softened butter and powdered sugar until light and fluffy. Mix in the vanilla extract.
   - Gradually add the flour and salt, mixing until the dough forms. Stir in the chopped nuts until evenly distributed.
2. **Shape the Cookies:**
   - Roll the dough into small balls, about 1 inch in

The Vintage Christmas Revival Guide

diameter. Place the cookies on a parchment-lined baking sheet.

3. **Bake:**
   - Preheat the oven to 180°C (350°F). Bake the cookies for 12-15 minutes, or until the bottoms are lightly golden. The tops should remain pale.
4. **Coat in Powdered Sugar:**
   - While the cookies are still warm, roll them in powdered sugar to coat. Let them cool completely, then roll them in powdered sugar again for a thick, snowy coating.

Snowball Cookies melt in your mouth and add a lovely, nostalgic charm to holiday cookie trays.

These classic **1960s & 1970s Christmas cookies** are a delightful way to bring a nostalgic touch to your holiday baking. Whether you're decorating gingerbread men and sugar cookies with family or rolling rum balls and snowball cookies in powdered sugar, these timeless treats capture the festive spirit and warmth of mid-century Christmas traditions.

Beverages: Mulled Wine & Classic Eggnog

No nostalgic Christmas celebration is complete without warming, festive drinks that bring comfort and joy to chilly winter nights. Classic beverages like **eggnog** and **mulled wine** have been cherished for centuries, evoking a sense of tradition and holiday spirit. With their rich flavours and cozy aromas, these drinks are perfect for family gatherings, holiday parties, or simply sipping by the fire. Below, we'll explore the history and recipes of eggnog and mulled wine, including non-alcoholic variations and the stories that have kept these drinks popular through the ages.

EGGNOG

Eggnog has long been associated with the holiday season, dating back to 17th-century England where it was enjoyed by the upper classes. Made with a rich blend of eggs, cream, sugar, and alcohol, it became a symbol of warmth and celebration. The drink made its way to America, where it became a festive favourite during Christmas. Today, eggnog is available in both alcoholic and non-alcoholic versions, enjoyed by families of all ages as they gather to celebrate the season.

Traditional Eggnog Recipe
Ingredients:

- 4 large eggs, separated
- 100g granulated sugar
- 500ml whole milk
- 250ml heavy cream
- 120ml rum, brandy, or bourbon (optional)
- 1 tsp vanilla extract
- Freshly grated nutmeg (for garnish)

Instructions:

1. **Whip the Egg Yolks:**
    - In a large mixing bowl, beat the egg yolks until they become light and fluffy. Gradually add the sugar, continuing to beat until the mixture is creamy and pale in colour.
2. **Add the Milk and Cream:**
    - Stir in the milk, heavy cream, and vanilla extract. If using alcohol, add the rum, brandy, or bourbon at this point. Whisk the mixture until smooth.

3. **Beat the Egg Whites:**
    - In a separate bowl, beat the egg whites until soft peaks form. Gently fold the egg whites into the eggnog mixture, creating a light and frothy texture.
4. **Chill and Serve:**
    - Refrigerate the eggnog for at least 1 hour to let the flavors develop. When ready to serve, ladle into cups and garnish with freshly grated nutmeg.

Non-Alcoholic Eggnog Recipe

For a family-friendly version of this classic holiday drink, simply omit the alcohol and follow the same steps. This variation allows everyone to enjoy the creamy, comforting taste of eggnog without the added spirits.

Ingredients:

- 4 large eggs, separated
- 100g granulated sugar
- 500ml whole milk
- 250ml heavy cream
- 1 tsp vanilla extract
- Freshly grated nutmeg (for garnish)

Instructions:

- Follow the same method as the traditional recipe, skipping the alcohol. You can also add a splash of vanilla or almond extract for an extra flavour boost. Chill and serve with a generous dusting of nutmeg on top.

MULLED WINE

Mulled wine has a long history in Europe, where it's been enjoyed as a festive winter drink for centuries. Originating in Roman times, the practice of warming wine with spices spread across Europe, where it became a holiday tradition, especially in countries like Germany, Sweden, and the UK. Known as **Glühwein** in Germany and **Glögg** in Scandinavia, mulled wine is a warming, spiced drink often served at Christmas markets and holiday gatherings. The combination of wine, citrus, and aromatic spices makes this drink a comforting choice during the cold winter months.

Mulled Wine Recipe
Ingredients:

- 1 bottle of red wine (such as Merlot or Cabernet Sauvignon)
- 1 orange, sliced
- 2 cinnamon sticks
- 5 whole cloves
- 2 star anise
- 2-3 tbsp honey or sugar (to taste)
- 60ml brandy (optional)
- 1/2 tsp freshly grated nutmeg
- Additional orange slices and cinnamon sticks (for garnish)

Instructions:

1. **Heat the Wine:**
   - In a large saucepan, combine the red wine, orange slices, cinnamon sticks, cloves, star anise, and

honey or sugar. Warm over medium heat, stirring occasionally. Be careful not to let the mixture boil, as this can cook off the alcohol.
2. **Simmer:**
   - Let the wine simmer gently for about 20 minutes, allowing the flavours to infuse. If you prefer a stronger drink, stir in the brandy at this point.
3. **Serve:**
   - Once the wine is warmed and fragrant, strain out the spices and orange slices. Ladle the mulled wine into mugs or heatproof glasses, and garnish with fresh orange slices and cinnamon sticks.

Non-Alcoholic Spiced Cider (Mulled Cider)

For those who prefer a non-alcoholic alternative, spiced cider is a perfect choice. This cozy drink is made with apple cider and the same warming spices used in mulled wine, offering a comforting, family-friendly option.

Ingredients:

- 1 liter apple cider
- 1 orange, sliced
- 2 cinnamon sticks
- 5 whole cloves
- 2 star anise
- 2 tbsp honey or brown sugar (to taste)
- 1/2 tsp freshly grated nutmeg

Instructions:

1. **Heat the Cider:**
   - In a large saucepan, combine the apple cider, orange slices, cinnamon sticks, cloves, star anise,

and honey or brown sugar. Warm over medium heat, stirring occasionally.

2. **Simmer:**
    - Let the cider simmer gently for 15-20 minutes to allow the flavours to meld together. Be sure not to boil.
3. **Serve:**
    - Strain out the spices and orange slices, and ladle the spiced cider into mugs. Garnish with a slice of orange or a cinnamon stick for a festive touch.

STORIES AND TRADITIONS **Behind These Drinks**

EGGNOG HAS roots in medieval Europe, where it was derived from a hot milk punch called **posset**. Over time, it evolved into a chilled, egg-based beverage enjoyed by the wealthy. In colonial America, rum was the spirit of choice for spiking eggnog, as it was more affordable than European wines and spirits. The drink became associated with Christmas celebrations as it was shared among family and friends during festive gatherings. Today, eggnog is a holiday staple, found in homes across the world in both traditional and non-alcoholic forms.

Mulled wine has a rich history dating back to ancient Rome, where wine was often heated with spices to make it last longer during cold winters. The practice spread through Europe, evolving into a cherished Christmas tradition. In Germany, **Glühwein** is a popular drink at holiday markets, while Sweden's **Glögg** is served with almonds and raisins. The aromatic spices used in mulled wine — cinnamon, cloves, star anise — are believed to have warming properties, making it a perfect drink to enjoy on cold December nights.

Both **mulled wine** and **spiced cider** offer a taste of European tradition, bringing warmth, comfort, and a sense of nostalgia to the holiday season. Whether you're gathered around the fire with friends or preparing for a Christmas party, these drinks are sure to fill your home with festive cheer and the sweet aromas of the holidays.

James Holloway

Classic beverages like **eggnog** *and* **mulled wine** *have been cherished for centuries, evoking a sense of tradition and holiday spirit.*

Part Two
Crafts: Handmade Christmas Decorations

One of the joys of Christmases past was the tradition of creating homemade decorations with simple, natural materials.

This section focuses on recreating that nostalgic magic by introducing charming crafts from different eras, each reflecting the unique style and aesthetic of its time.

These crafts are not only beautiful and timeless but offer a way to slow down and savour the process of making your home festive.

Victorian Christmas Crafts

The Victorian era is known for its opulent holiday decor, but it was also a time when families crafted many of their own ornaments and decorations by hand. Using natural elements like fruits, greenery, and paper, these traditional Victorian crafts add a touch of timeless elegance to any home.

Orange and Clove Pomanders

Pomanders were a beloved Victorian tradition, filling homes with the warm, spiced scent of the holidays. These fragrant decorations were often hung on trees or placed around the house to provide a festive aroma that would last through the season. Making them is a simple yet sensory experience.

Materials:

- Fresh oranges (or other citrus like lemons or limes)
- Whole cloves
- Ribbon (for hanging)

- Toothpick or skewer (optional, to help pierce the orange skin)

Instructions:

1. **Start with the oranges**: Select firm, fresh oranges that are small to medium in size.
2. **Pierce the skin**: Using a toothpick or skewer, poke holes in the orange skin to make it easier to insert the cloves. If you prefer a more rustic look, you can skip this step and simply press the cloves directly into the orange.
3. **Insert the cloves**: Push a clove into each hole until it's securely in place. You can create patterns—spirals, stripes, or random clusters—or cover the entire orange in cloves for a more intense fragrance.
4. **Wrap with ribbon**: Once your orange is studded with cloves, wrap a ribbon around it in a cross pattern (like a gift), tying it at the top. This will give you a loop to hang the pomander on your tree or mantel.
5. **Let it dry**: Over time, the orange will dry out and shrink slightly, intensifying the aroma and creating a lovely, vintage appearance. The pomander can last for weeks, making it an enduring part of your holiday decor.

VICTORIAN PAPER SNOWFLAKES

VICTORIANS LOVED the art of paper cutting, and **paper snowflakes** were a favourite craft for decorating windows and Christmas trees. They are simple to make and bring a nostalgic charm to your holiday decor, casting delicate patterns of light and shadow when hung near a window.

Materials:

- White or coloured paper (thin enough for easy cutting)
- Scissors
- String or thread for hanging

Instructions:

1. **Fold the paper**: Begin with a square piece of paper. Fold it in half diagonally to form a triangle. Fold the triangle in half again, and then once more to create a smaller, thinner triangle.
2. **Cut the edges**: Using scissors, carefully cut small shapes along the folded edges of the paper—triangles, half circles, and small squares work well. You can experiment with different designs to create unique patterns.
3. **Unfold**: Once you've finished cutting, gently unfold the paper to reveal your snowflake. Each one will be unique!
4. **Hang or display**: Use a small piece of thread or ribbon to hang your snowflakes from the ceiling, in front of a window, or on the Christmas tree. You can also string several together to create a snowflake garland.

James Holloway

Victorian Paper Snowflakes

Simple Salt Dough Ornaments

SALT DOUGH IS a versatile material that has been used for crafting decorations for centuries. These **salt dough ornaments** are easy to make and can be customised with different shapes and colours, making them a perfect craft for both children and adults.

Materials:

- 2 cups all-purpose flour
- 1 cup salt
- 1 cup water
- Cookie cutters (holiday shapes like stars, trees, or hearts)
- Acrylic paints or food colouring (optional)
- Ribbon or twine for hanging

Instructions:

1. **Make the dough**: In a large bowl, mix together the flour and salt. Gradually add the water, stirring until a dough forms. If it's too sticky, add more flour; if it's too dry, add more water.
2. **Roll out the dough**: On a lightly floured surface, roll out the dough to about 1/4 inch thick.
3. **Cut out shapes**: Use cookie cutters to cut festive shapes like stars, hearts, trees, or bells. You can also use a toothpick to press designs into the surface of the dough or create texture.
4. **Make a hole for hanging**: Use a straw or skewer to poke a small hole near the top of each ornament for threading the ribbon later.

5. **Bake**: Preheat the oven to 200°F (93°C). Place the dough shapes on a baking sheet and bake for 2-3 hours, or until completely hardened. Allow them to cool.
6. **Decorate**: Once cool, you can paint your ornaments using acrylic paints, or keep them plain for a more rustic look. You can also add glitter or press small beads or buttons into the dough before baking for extra flair.
7. **Hang**: Thread a ribbon or twine through the hole and hang the ornaments on your tree, garland, or wreath.

CANDLE HOLDERS and Traditional Wreaths

THE VICTORIANS LOVED natural greenery during the holidays, and wreaths were a centrepiece of their decorations. By incorporating dried fruits and fresh greenery, you can make a **Victorian-inspired wreath** that is both beautiful and fragrant. Candle holders made with greenery were also common and added a festive glow to holiday tables.

Materials for Wreath:

- Fresh greenery (pine, fir, holly, or ivy)
- Dried fruits (such as orange slices, cinnamon sticks, or cranberries)
- Floral wire or twine
- Wreath frame (either store-bought or made from pliable branches)
- Ribbon for hanging

Instructions for Wreath:

1. **Prepare the greenery**: Gather fresh greenery, trimming it into manageable pieces. If you're using a mix of pine, fir, and holly, alternate the types for a more textured wreath.
2. **Attach greenery to the frame**: Using floral wire or twine, attach the greenery to the wreath frame by wrapping it around small bundles of greens and securing them to the base.
3. **Add dried fruit and accents**: Once the wreath is fully covered in greenery, tuck in dried fruit slices, cinnamon sticks, or berries. Use wire or hot glue to secure them in place.

4. **Hang and enjoy**: Tie a ribbon at the top and hang your wreath on your front door or above the mantel for an authentic Victorian touch.

These simple yet elegant Victorian crafts evoke the beauty of a bygone era, adding a timeless charm to your holiday celebrations.

1950s & 1960s Christmas Crafts

The mid-20th century brought about a new era of Christmas decor, characterised by bright colors, shiny metallics, and bold, playful designs. Crafts from this period often incorporated synthetic materials like felt and tinsel, reflecting the space-age optimism of the time. These easy-to-make decorations capture the retro charm of the 1950s and 1960s, perfect for adding a playful, nostalgic touch to your Christmas celebrations.

James Holloway

Vintage-Style Felt Ornaments

Felt ornaments were hugely popular in the 1950s and 1960s because they were easy to make, durable, and colourful. This craft is a great opportunity to get creative with simple materials like felt, buttons, and sequins, making fun, personalised ornaments for your tree.

Materials:

- Felt sheets in various colours
- Scissors
- Needle and thread or fabric glue
- Buttons, sequins, beads
- Ribbon or string for hanging
- Cotton or polyester stuffing (optional, if making 3D ornaments)

Instructions:

1. **Cut out your shapes**: Choose classic Christmas shapes like stars, trees, bells, or stockings. Cut out two identical pieces from your felt for each ornament (one for the front and one for the back).
2. **Decorate**: Before stitching or gluing the two sides together, decorate one side with buttons, sequins, or beads. You can create designs like Christmas tree lights, polka dots, or stripes using these embellishments. If you're using glue, let it dry completely before moving on to the next step.

3. **Sew or glue the ornament**: Place the two felt pieces together and either sew them with a blanket stitch around the edges or glue them together with fabric glue. If you want a 3D effect, stuff a little cotton or polyester filling inside before sealing the edges.
4. **Add a hanger**: Sew or glue a small loop of ribbon or string to the top of the ornament so you can hang it on your tree.
5. **Personalise**: If you want to go the extra mile, personalise the ornament by stitching or gluing on initials, dates, or holiday messages.

Tinsel Garlands

NOTHING SAYS mid-century Christmas quite like a sparkly **tinsel garland**. While modern garlands are often pre-made, making your own tinsel garland at home is a fun, nostalgic activity. It's a simple way to bring a little retro flair to your holiday decor.

MATERIALS:

- Thin wire or string (for the base)
- Tinsel or metallic yarn (in silver, gold, or any colour of your choice)
- Scissors

Instructions:

1. **Create the base**: Cut a length of thin wire or string as long as you want your garland to be. If you're using wire, you can bend and shape it into fun patterns, like spirals or zigzags.
2. **Attach the tinsel**: Cut your tinsel or metallic yarn into small pieces, about 2-3 inches long. Take one piece at a time and tie it or twist it around the wire or string, spacing each piece evenly as you work your way along the base. If using string, you can also secure the tinsel pieces with small dots of hot glue.
3. **Fluff and trim**: Once you've covered the length of your base, fluff up the tinsel to create a full, sparkly effect. Trim any uneven pieces to achieve a uniform look.

4. **Hang the garland**: Drape your garland over the tree, across the mantel, or around doorways for that shimmering retro holiday vibe.

Glitter-Covered Pinecones

Glitter-covered pinecones were a quintessential holiday craft of the mid-century era, adding sparkle to natural elements in a way that reflected the era's love for combining traditional and modern styles. This simple craft is perfect for children and adults alike, and the results are a festive combination of rustic charm and glitzy glamour.

Materials:

- Pinecones (collected or store-bought)
- White craft glue or Mod Podge
- Glitter (silver, gold, or multicolored)
- Ribbon or string for hanging (optional)
- Small paintbrush

Instructions:

1. **Prepare the pinecones**: If you've collected the pinecones yourself, make sure they're clean and dry. You can bake them in the oven at a low temperature for 30 minutes to ensure they're bug-free and open.
2. **Apply glue**: Using a small paintbrush, apply a thin layer of glue or Mod Podge to the edges of the pinecone scales. You can cover as much or as little of the pinecone as you like—whether you want just a dusting of glitter or a full-on sparkle fest.
3. **Add glitter**: Sprinkle glitter over the glued areas, making sure to cover them completely. Shake off any excess glitter onto a piece of paper, which you can reuse for the next pinecone.
4. **Let it dry**: Allow the pinecones to dry completely. Once dry, you can either leave them as is for a tabletop

display or attach a ribbon or string to the top to hang them on your tree.
5. **Optional Variation**: If you want to go full retro, consider adding a touch of spray snow to the tips of the pinecones for an extra wintry look.

Glitter-Covered Pinecones

Retro Tree Topper

The Christmas tree topper is the crowning glory of the tree, and during the 1950s and 1960s, tree toppers were often made from space-age materials like foil and wire, reflecting the atomic style of the era. This **DIY retro tree topper** is a fun project that brings that vintage flair back to your holiday decor.

Materials:

- Foil or metallic paper (silver or gold)
- Craft wire (medium gauge)
- Scissors
- Hot glue gun
- Ribbon or tinsel (optional)

INSTRUCTIONS:

1. **Create the star shape**: Cut out two identical star shapes from your foil or metallic paper. Stars with sharp, elongated points were popular in the mid-century era, so feel free to exaggerate the star's points for that retro look.
2. **Attach wire**: Cut a length of wire that will serve as the "stem" of the tree topper, allowing it to sit snugly at the top of your tree. Use the hot glue gun to secure one end of the wire to the back of one of the star shapes.
3. **Assemble the topper**: Glue the second star shape on top of the first, sandwiching the wire in between. If you want to make the star more three-dimensional, you can bend the points slightly outward and add a little stuffing or another piece of metallic paper inside.
4. **Embellish**: For an extra touch of 1950s glam, wrap a small piece of tinsel or metallic ribbon around the base of the star, or glue small sequins or beads onto the star's surface for added sparkle.
5. **Place on the tree**: Once your tree topper is complete, wind the wire around the top of your tree, ensuring the star sits securely at the very top.

THESE MID-CENTURY MODERN CRAFTS, with their vibrant colours, metallics, and playful designs, capture the whimsy and innovation of 1950s and 1960s holiday decor. Each project is a fun way to bring a touch of retro style to your Christmas celebrations, creating a festive, nostalgic atmosphere in your home.

Scandinavian & Folk-Inspired Crafts

Scandinavian Christmas traditions emphasize simplicity, natural materials, and handmade items, reflecting a deep connection to nature and family. Folk-inspired crafts, often passed down through generations, are typically made from felt, straw, and wood, and celebrate the warm, rustic charm of the holiday season. These Scandinavian and folk-inspired crafts are perfect for bringing a cozy, old-world feel to your home, with designs that are both timeless and meaningful.

James Holloway

DIY Woven Paper Heart Baskets (Julehjerter)

ONE OF THE most iconic Scandinavian Christmas decorations is the **woven paper heart basket**, or "Julehjerter." Traditionally made in Denmark, these charming paper hearts are often filled with sweets or small treats and hung on the Christmas tree. The baskets are easy to make and add a touch of Nordic tradition to your decor.

Materials:

- Two sheets of sturdy coloured paper (in contrasting colours, such as red and white)
- Scissors
- Pencil
- Ruler

Instructions:

1. **Cut the paper**: Begin by cutting two rectangles of equal size from the coloured paper, about 3x9 inches each. These will form the basket. Fold each rectangle in half lengthwise, creating a 3x4.5 inch folded shape.
2. **Draw and cut the rounded tops**: On the folded edge of each rectangle, draw a half-circle at the top, starting about 1.5 inches from the fold. Cut along this line to create the rounded tops of your heart shape.
3. **Create the weaving strips**: With the rectangles still folded, cut three evenly spaced slits from the folded edge up towards the curved top, stopping about 1/4 inch from the edge. Be sure both rectangles have the same number of cuts and slits of the same width.

4. **Weave the heart**: Now comes the weaving! Take the two pieces of paper and interweave them. Slide the first strip of one piece over and under the strips of the other piece, alternating the pattern to create a checkerboard effect. The woven strips will form a heart-shaped pocket.
5. **Finish and hang**: Once the heart is fully woven, trim any rough edges. You can attach a small loop of ribbon to the top of the heart and hang it on your Christmas tree, or fill it with candy and give it as a sweet treat for guests.

Hand-Stitched Felt Ornaments with Folk Art Designs

SCANDINAVIAN-INSPIRED **hand-stitched felt ornaments** often feature simple, elegant designs that reflect traditional folk art motifs like stars, snowflakes, and hearts. These felt decorations are easy to make, and their homespun charm adds a cozy, personal touch to your tree or holiday decor.

Materials:

- Felt sheets in various colours (red, white, green, blue)
- Embroidery thread in contrasting colours
- Needle
- Scissors
- Chalk or fabric pen (for drawing designs)
- Ribbon or string for hanging
- Cotton or polyester stuffing (optional, for 3D effect)

Instructions:

1. **Cut the felt shapes**: Cut two identical shapes out of the felt. Popular folk art shapes include hearts, stars, Christmas trees, and bells. You can make these as flat ornaments or add a bit of stuffing for a 3D look.
2. **Decorate with embroidery**: Using embroidery thread, stitch simple designs onto one of the felt pieces. Popular folk art patterns include small flowers, stars, or geometric shapes. Use contrasting thread colours to make the designs pop. For example, white thread on red felt creates a classic Scandinavian look.
3. **Sew the ornament together**: Once your design is complete, place the two felt pieces together and stitch around the edges with a blanket stitch. If you're

making a 3D ornament, leave a small opening, stuff the ornament lightly, and then finish stitching the edges closed.
4. **Add a hanger**: Sew a small loop of ribbon or thread to the top of the ornament to hang it on your tree or as part of a garland.
5. **Personalise**: You can also add initials, dates, or small holiday messages to make these ornaments personalised keepsakes.

Hand-Stitched Felt Ornaments with Folk Art Designs

James Holloway

STRAW ORNAMENTS and Wooden Stars

STRAW ORNAMENTS ARE an essential part of Scandinavian Christmas traditions, symbolising the importance of nature and simplicity. These rustic decorations, often shaped like stars, angels, or animals, are made from dried straw and represent the harvest and the return of light during the dark winter months. **Wooden stars**, similarly, offer a timeless, old-world charm that harkens back to traditional craftsmanship.

MATERIALS FOR STRAW ORNAMENTS:

- Straw (available at craft stores or online)
- Thread or fine wire
- Scissors
- Ruler
- Needle

Instructions for Straw Ornaments:

1. **Prepare the straw**: If your straw is dry and stiff, soak it in warm water for about 30 minutes to make it more pliable. Once it's flexible, pat it dry with a towel.
2. **Cut the straw**: Cut the straw into equal lengths, usually about 4-6 inches long, depending on the size of the ornament you wish to make. You will need 8-12 pieces for a basic star ornament.
3. **Assemble the star**: Lay out the straw pieces in a crisscross pattern to form a star shape, with the ends fanning out evenly. Use thin thread or wire to bind the

centre of the straw pieces tightly, securing them in place.
4. **Secure and embellish**: Once the star is bound together in the centre, trim the ends of the straw to make the points even. You can leave the ornament plain for a rustic look or add small beads or red thread to the ends of the points for a festive touch.
5. **Hang**: Attach a loop of thread to one of the points of the star for hanging on the tree or as part of a garland.

Materials for Wooden Stars:

- Thin wood sheets (balsa or craft wood)
- Small saw or craft knife (if cutting by hand)
- Sandpaper (fine grit)
- Wood glue
- Paint (optional, for decoration)
- Twine or ribbon for hanging

Instructions for Wooden Stars:

1. **Cut the star shape**: If you have a template, use it to trace star shapes onto the wood sheet. Cut out the stars using a small saw or craft knife. If you're cutting by hand, make sure to work slowly and carefully. Sand the edges of each star until smooth.
2. **Decorate the stars**: You can leave the stars plain for a minimalist look, or paint them in simple, folk-inspired colours like red, white, or gold. If you prefer a natural look, a light coat of beeswax or wood oil will enhance the grain of the wood.
3. **Assemble multiple stars**: For a 3D effect, you

can glue two wooden stars together at a slight angle, creating depth and visual interest.
4. **Hang**: Attach a small loop of twine or ribbon to the top of each star, and hang them on your tree, in the window, or as part of a larger holiday display.

These Scandinavian and folk-inspired crafts embrace the warmth and simplicity of traditional holiday celebrations. Whether you're weaving paper heart baskets, stitching felt ornaments, or crafting straw stars, these projects bring a cozy, homespun charm to your Christmas decor, honouring the timeless beauty of old-world craftsmanship.

Part Three
Decor: Transforming Your Home into a Cozy Christmas Haven

One of the most enchanting aspects of Christmas is the way we decorate our homes to reflect the warmth and beauty of the season.

In this chapter, we'll explore how to capture the nostalgic charm of Christmases past by recreating the look and feel of vintage holiday decor.

From lush Victorian-inspired opulence to the subtle beauty of traditional materials, these ideas will help you transform your home into a cozy Christmas haven.

Victorian-Inspired Christmas Decor

The Victorian era is synonymous with Christmas nostalgia. It was during this period that many of the traditions and decorations we associate with the holiday took root, including the opulent and elaborate decor styles that reflect the era's love for beauty and richness. Victorian-inspired Christmas decor is all about embracing lavish detail, rich colour palettes, and natural materials, all of which combine to create a warm, elegant, and timeless holiday atmosphere.

1. Lush, Opulent Mantelpieces

A Victorian mantelpiece decorated for Christmas was often a true work of art, featuring an abundance of greenery, candles, and luxurious accents. To recreate this look, focus on layering textures and incorporating both natural elements and ornate accessories.

Materials & Suggestions:

- **Greenery**: Start with a lush base of fresh or faux greenery like pine, fir, or ivy draped across the mantel.

For added authenticity, you could also incorporate sprigs of holly with its bright red berries. Victorian decor often used real greenery, which gave the home a fragrant, festive scent.

- **Candles**: Candles in brass holders were a hallmark of Victorian Christmas decor, symbolising warmth and light during the long winter nights. Arrange tall brass candlesticks along the mantelpiece, interspersed between the greenery. If you prefer a safer option, battery-operated candles with flickering lights can recreate the same cozy glow.
- **Accents**: Add depth and luxury to your mantel with accents like ornate glass ornaments, gilded picture frames, and antique-inspired trinkets. Victorian Christmases celebrated detail, so don't be afraid to mix and match textures and metallics—brass, gold, and silver work beautifully together.
- **Ribbons & Bows**: Finish the mantel with wide velvet or satin ribbons, tied in large bows or draped elegantly through the greenery. Deep jewel tones like burgundy, forest green, and midnight blue add a regal touch.

The Vintage Christmas Revival Guide

Candles in brass holders were a hallmark of Victorian Christmas decor, symbolizing warmth and light during the long winter nights.

2. Layering Fabrics: Velvets, Lace, and Brocades

A Victorian home at Christmas would have been rich with luxurious fabrics that added warmth and elegance. You can achieve this same effect by incorporating sumptuous layers of textiles throughout your home decor.

FABRICS & Color Palette:

- **Velvet**: Drape rich, plush velvet throws over armchairs and sofas. Choose deep colours like ruby red, emerald green, and royal blue. Velvet not only adds a touch of luxury but also warmth and texture, perfect for the cozy atmosphere of Christmas.
- **Lace**: Victorian homes often used lace as an accent to soften and refine decor. You can lay delicate lace tablecloths or runners on your dining table or drape lace curtains in windows. The intricate patterns will add a timeless elegance to your Christmas setting.

- **Brocade and Damask**: For a truly Victorian feel, incorporate brocade or damask pillows and table settings in rich, jewel-toned patterns. These fabrics, known for their ornate, raised designs, bring a sense of grandeur to your decor.
- **Colour Palette**: Stick to traditional Victorian Christmas colours—deep reds, golds, and forest greens are ideal for capturing the era's rich and opulent vibe. Accents of royal blue or silver can add depth and contrast to the colour scheme.

3. Creating a Victorian-Inspired Christmas Tree

The Christmas tree became a staple of holiday decor during the Victorian era, and Queen Victoria and Prince Albert are credited with popularising the tradition in the mid-19th century. A Victorian-inspired Christmas tree is lush, elegant, and filled with handmade or ornate decorations. Here's how you can bring that traditional charm into your home.

Decorating the Tree:

- **Paper Chains & Ornaments**: One of the most nostalgic Victorian tree decorations is the paper chain, which was often handmade by families. To recreate this, use strips of red and green paper to make simple paper chains that add a pop of colour and a personal touch to your tree. Victorian children would often make salt dough or paper ornaments, so consider adding these handmade items for a truly authentic look.

- **Candles (Battery-Operated)**: In the Victorian era, candles were often used to light the Christmas tree. While real candles are a fire hazard, battery-operated candles can give you the same warm, flickering effect without the danger. Place these evenly around the tree, nestled among the branches.
- **Glass Ornaments**: Victorian trees were often adorned with delicate glass ornaments, which were typically hand-blown and intricately designed. You can find reproductions of these ornaments, or look for vintage pieces that feature charming designs like angels, birds, or fruits. Glass icicles also add a touch of sparkle.
- **Natural Decorations**: In true Victorian fashion, incorporate natural elements into your tree decor. Dried oranges, cinnamon sticks, and pinecones are not only beautiful but bring a fragrant, old-world charm to the tree. You can also hang small clusters of berries, gilded walnuts, or strings of popcorn for an authentic look.
- **Ribbons & Garlands**: Instead of modern tinsel, use long strands of velvet or satin ribbon in rich colours to wrap around the tree. You can also drape garlands of beads or cranberries for a festive touch. The goal is to create a tree that is both opulent and cozy, filled with textures and warm colours.

The Tree Topper: For the finishing touch, top your tree with a traditional Victorian-style ornament. This could be a star made from gilded metal or glass, or an angel dressed in delicate lace. Victorian tree toppers were often ornate and symbolic, representing the star of Bethlehem or the guiding angel.

. . .

4. Additional Victorian Decor Tips

- **Doorways and Windows**: Drape greenery over doorways and windows, adorned with velvet ribbons and small glass ornaments. Victorian homes often had wreaths or garlands hung on every available surface, creating a lush, festive environment.
- **Tables-capes**: When setting your holiday table, think of layers and opulence. Use fine china, crystal goblets, and silver cutlery, if available. Set the table with a rich velvet or lace runner, and top it with brass candlesticks and a centrepiece made of fresh greenery and dried fruits.
- **Lighting**: In addition to candles, Victorian homes made use of oil lamps and gas lights. While these might not be practical today, you can recreate the soft, glowing effect with modern table lamps or lanterns, adding a layer of warmth to your holiday decor.

A Victorian-inspired Christmas home is all about indulgence in detail and creating a warm, inviting space filled with the richness of natural and handmade elements. By focusing on layers of texture, luxurious fabrics, and opulent decorations, you can recreate the nostalgic charm of a Victorian Christmas that brings beauty, warmth, and a sense of timeless tradition to your holiday celebrations.

Mid-Century Modern Christmas

The mid-20th century brought an entirely new approach to holiday decor, reflecting the bold, optimistic spirit of the post-war era. Mid-century modern Christmas decor was a celebration of innovation, embracing bright colours, sleek lines, and futuristic designs that perfectly captured the atomic age's enthusiasm. Leaning into this retro style can bring a playful, nostalgic vibe to your Christmas decor while adding a touch of vintage glamour.

1. Retro Aluminium Christmas Trees

Perhaps the most iconic symbol of mid-century modern Christmas decor is the **aluminium Christmas tree**. Introduced in the late 1950s, these trees became wildly popular throughout the 1960s for their space-age aesthetic, shimmering silver branches, and modern flair. While authentic vintage aluminium trees can still be found in thrift stores or online, there are also high-quality reproductions available today that capture the same dazzling appeal.

. . .

How to Style Your Aluminium Tree:

- **Colour Wheel Lights**: Aluminium trees were often paired with **colour wheel lights**, which cast rotating shades of red, blue, green, and yellow over the reflective branches. You can find reproductions of these colour wheels, or you can create a similar effect with modern colour-changing LED spotlights aimed at the tree. The rotating lights bring movement and magic, making the tree shimmer in different hues.
- **Vintage Ornaments**: Decorate your aluminium tree with vintage or retro-inspired ornaments, preferably in bold, glossy colours. Glass ornaments in metallic finishes—gold, pink, blue, or even turquoise—are ideal for creating that mid-century modern look. Geometric shapes, starbursts, and atomic motifs were all popular themes during this period.
- **Minimalist Approach**: The sleek, metallic beauty of an aluminium tree often meant that it was sparsely decorated compared to traditional evergreen trees. Allow the tree's shimmering branches to take centre stage by limiting your ornament selection to a few well-placed, colourful pieces.

2. Bold Colours and Starburst Motifs

Mid-century modern decor embraced bold, contrasting colours and geometric shapes, which translated into a fun and festive approach to holiday decorating. Incorporating these elements into your Christmas decor brings a sense of nostalgia and energy to your home.

INCORPORATING BOLD COLOURS:

- **Accent Colours**: Bold colours like bright turquoise, hot pink, orange, or lime green were staples of mid-century decor. Incorporate these shades into your Christmas colour palette by using them for your ornaments, table settings, or throw pillows. You can mix them with traditional reds and greens or use them on their own for a modern twist on holiday cheer.
- **Colourful Garlands**: Consider adding brightly coloured tinsel or pom-pom garlands to your Christmas tree, mantel, or doorways. These whimsical touches echo the playfulness of mid-century style.

Starburst Motifs and Sputnik-Style Decorations:

- **Starburst Ornaments**: The starburst was an iconic mid-century motif that fit perfectly into the futuristic, atomic aesthetic of the time. You can easily incorporate this design into your holiday decor by finding or crafting starburst-shaped ornaments or tree toppers. Look for ornaments that feature metallic rays shooting out from a central point, mimicking the starburst or Sputnik-style chandeliers that were popular in mid-century homes.
- **Sputnik-Inspired Decor**: In addition to ornaments, you can add Sputnik-style touches with metallic wreaths, wall art, or even DIY projects like constructing a Sputnik-style tree topper using wire

and shiny metallic balls. These decorations evoke the era's fascination with space exploration and modern design, adding a sleek, stylish touch to your holiday decor.

3. Classic Mid-Century Christmas Lights

Twinkling lights are a Christmas decor essential, and the mid-century era brought about some iconic lighting styles that are still beloved today. However, vintage lights require special care to ensure safety, so here's how to recreate the look while keeping modern safety standards in mind.

C7 AND C9 BULBS:

- **Large Bulbs**: One of the most recognisable mid-century Christmas light styles is the C7 and C9 bulb strings. These large, colourful lights—often in reds, greens, blues, and yellows—were a staple of 1950s and 1960s outdoor and indoor Christmas displays. Today, you can find reproductions of these lights in both their original incandescent form and as safer, more energy-efficient LEDs.
- **Displaying Vintage Lights Safely**: If you're lucky enough to have original vintage lights, make sure to check for frayed wires, broken bulbs, or other signs of wear before plugging them in. It's a good idea to replace the old cords or sockets with modern ones, or consider using the vintage lights purely for decoration without plugging them in to avoid any risk of fire or electrical issues.

Vintage lights require special care to ensure safety

Bubble Lights:

- **Retro Bubble Lights**: Another mid-century favourite was the **bubble light**, which featured a small vial of liquid that would bubble when the light warmed up. These lights are still available today, both in vintage form and as reproductions. Bubble lights add a fun, nostalgic touch to your tree or mantel display, bringing a bit of kinetic energy to your decor.

Safety Tip: When using any Christmas lights, especially vintage or reproduction styles, always check that they are UL-certified and rated for indoor or outdoor use (depending on where you plan to display them). Never overload electrical outlets, and consider using surge protectors or timers to minimise risk.

4. Additional Mid-Century Decor Tips

- **Retro Stockings**: Hang stockings that feature fun, mid-century patterns, such as atomic stars, retro

reindeer, or bold geometric shapes. You can find retro-inspired stockings at vintage stores or make your own using bright-coloured felt and embroidery.
- **Festive Bar Cart**: The mid-century era was also famous for its cocktail culture, so why not incorporate a **holiday-themed bar cart** into your decor? Stock it with vintage glassware, holiday cocktail recipes, and festive garnishes like candy canes, cranberries, and sprigs of rosemary. For an extra touch of retro, add a small tinsel tree or starburst decor piece on the cart.
- **Holiday Dinnerware**: Complete the mid-century look by setting your holiday table with vintage or retro-style dinnerware. Look for patterns featuring atomic stars, boomerangs, or holiday motifs in bold colours. A vintage ceramic Christmas tree centrepiece will add an extra dose of nostalgia to your table.

A MID-CENTURY modern Christmas is all about embracing the bold, futuristic design elements of the 1950s and 1960s. By incorporating retro aluminium trees, starburst motifs, and colourful vintage lights, you can create a vibrant, playful holiday atmosphere that captures the magic of this iconic era. Whether you're decorating with a minimalist approach or going all out with Sputnik-style ornaments, this nostalgic decor will bring mid-century charm to your Christmas celebrations.

Cozy Rustic & Cottage Christmas

The rustic and cottage-inspired Christmas decor brings to life the simpler, cozier aspects of the holiday season. It embraces natural elements, handmade touches, and a sense of warmth and tradition. This style of decorating is perfect for creating a welcoming, homey atmosphere that feels like a comforting embrace on a cold winter's day.

THINK OF HANDMADE QUILTS, mismatched china, and the soft glow of candlelight illuminating natural greenery, as these details make your home feel charming and timeless.

1. Embrace the Warmth of Handmade Textiles

In a rustic or cottage-style Christmas, textiles play a central role in creating a cozy and inviting atmosphere. Handmade quilts, tartan blankets, and soft pillows in rich, warm colours make every corner of your home feel welcoming.

. . .

How to Use Textiles in Your Decor:

- **Handmade Quilts**: Drape vintage or handmade quilts over the back of couches, armchairs, or even on the foot of your bed to create a cozy, lived-in feel. Quilts with holiday colours or traditional patchwork designs can serve as both practical and decorative pieces, adding warmth and texture to your space.
- **Tartan Blankets**: Nothing says rustic Christmas like the classic charm of tartan plaid. Use tartan blankets and throws in shades of red, green, and cream to bring a festive, traditional touch to your decor. These can be used on couches, chairs, or even as table runners for a holiday feast.
- **Wooden Figurines and Handcrafted Accents**: Include rustic, hand-carved wooden figurines like reindeer, snowmen, or simple wooden stars in your decor. These timeless pieces can be placed on mantels, shelves, or as centrepieces for your dining table.

2. Mason Jar Candle Holders and String Lights

Incorporating simple, everyday materials into your decor gives your home that charming, rustic Christmas aesthetic. Mason jars and string lights are perfect for creating a warm, glowing ambiance reminiscent of country cottages and rustic retreats.

Mason Jar Candle Holders:

- **How to Make**: Fill mason jars with a bit of Epsom salt or sand to create a snowy base, then place small tea lights or battery-operated candles inside. The

flickering glow from the candle inside the glass creates a soft, intimate light that feels like a cozy fireside glow.
- **Decorative Touches**: Tie a piece of twine or ribbon around the neck of the jar and add a sprig of evergreen, holly, or a cinnamon stick for a festive touch. You can line these jars up along windowsills, mantels, or use them as part of your table centrepiece.

String Lights:

- **Rustic Elegance**: String lights, especially warm white or soft amber lights, can transform a space into a magical winter wonderland. Drape them around wooden beams, windows, or inside woven baskets filled with pinecones and greenery to create a warm, welcoming glow.
- **Simple and Natural**: For a rustic twist, consider wrapping string lights around a grapevine wreath or along a wooden ladder leaned against the wall. The combination of the warm lights and natural materials adds an authentic cottage feel to your holiday decor.

3. Woven Baskets Filled with Pinecones and Greenery

Woven baskets filled with natural elements are a staple of rustic and cottage Christmas decor. These arrangements add a simple, earthy charm that brings the beauty of the outdoors inside, connecting you to nature and evoking the spirit of traditional Christmases.

How to Style Woven Baskets:

- **Fill with Pinecones**: Gather pinecones (either collected or store-bought) and fill a woven basket or a wooden crate. Add sprigs of evergreen or eucalyptus for a fresh, woodsy scent, and a few red berries for a pop of coulor.
- **Candles and Greenery**: You can place a large pillar candle in the centre of the basket, surrounded by greenery like cedar, pine, or fir branches. The contrast between the rustic wood of the basket and the vibrant greenery creates a simple yet stunning holiday display.
- **Mix with Ornaments**: For a festive touch, add a few vintage-style ornaments, jingle bells, or small holiday figurines to the basket arrangement. This combination of natural and decorative elements embodies the cozy, homey feel of cottage-style decor.

4. Setting a Rustic Holiday Table

For an rustic holiday table, incorporate antique or vintage pieces into your decor

The rustic and cottage-style Christmas table is all about warmth, charm, and an eclectic mix of vintage and handmade pieces. It's a celebration of simplicity and personal touches, creating an atmosphere that invites loved ones to gather around and enjoy good food and company.

Ideas for Setting a Rustic Holiday Table:

- **Mismatched China**: Rather than opting for a perfectly matching set of dishes, embrace the beauty of mismatched china. Mix and match vintage plates, bowls, and glasses in complementary colours and patterns to create a charming, relaxed holiday table. Look for dishes with floral or traditional holiday motifs, or simply mix soft colours like cream, green, and red for a festive yet understated look.
- **Vintage Napkins**: Add a touch of nostalgia with vintage napkins made from linen or cotton. You can tie them with twine or ribbon and tuck in a sprig of

rosemary or a small cinnamon stick for a fragrant, seasonal touch.
- **Simple Centrepieces**: A rustic table centrepiece doesn't need to be elaborate. Consider filling a wooden tray with fresh greenery, a few pinecones, and pillar candles. You can also place a large mason jar filled with fresh cranberries and water, topped with floating tea lights, for a simple, natural centrepiece that celebrates the season's bounty.
- **Natural Elements**: Scatter pinecones, acorns, or small sprigs of greenery along the table to bring the outdoors in. Wooden cutting boards or rustic trays can be used to serve bread or appetizers, adding to the organic, homey feel of the table setting.
- **Homespun Details**: Personalize the table with small, homespun details like handwritten place cards on kraft paper, tied with twine. You can also use simple wood slices as coasters or plate chargers for an extra rustic touch.

5. Additional Rustic & Cottage Decor Tips

- **Soft Lighting**: Create a warm, inviting ambiance by using plenty of candles throughout your home. Soft lighting is essential for the rustic look, so opt for warm, golden tones rather than bright white lights.
- **Natural Wreaths**: Hang natural wreaths made of grapevines, pine branches, or eucalyptus on your doors and windows. Decorate them with pinecones, dried orange slices, or simple ribbon for a festive, understated look.
- **Antique Furniture and Accessories**: Incorporate antique or vintage pieces into your decor,

like an old wooden sled propped up near the tree or an antique rocking chair draped with a quilt. These pieces add character and nostalgia, enhancing the cozy cottage feel.

A rustic table centerpiece doesn't need to be elaborate

A rustic and cottage-inspired Christmas is all about creating a warm, inviting environment that reflects the simple beauty of nature and the personal touches of handmade decor. By using natural materials, soft lighting, and vintage-inspired elements, you can transform your home into a peaceful, cozy retreat that evokes the charm of traditional, homespun holiday celebrations. Whether it's a table set with mismatched china or the soft glow of mason jar candles, this style brings the timeless magic of Christmas to life.

Holiday Traditions to Bring Back
Explore forgotten or lesser-known Christmas traditions from different eras and regions

The Vintage Christmas Revival Guide

As the holiday season approaches, many of us find ourselves seeking ways to make Christmas feel more meaningful, more personal, and more connected to the heart of the celebration. In our fast-paced world, it's easy to let traditions slip by the wayside, but these rituals are often what make the holiday season so special.

This chapter is a journey through forgotten or lesser-known Christmas customs from various eras and regions.

By reviving these charming practices, you can infuse your holiday celebrations with a deeper sense of warmth, history, and community.

The Charm of Old Traditions

Christmas is a time to slow down and savour the moments shared with loved ones. In days gone by, holiday traditions brought people together, creating memories that lasted a lifetime. The beauty of these customs lies in their simplicity. They remind us of the joy found in gathering around a fire, sharing stories, singing carols, or enjoying a quiet cup of tea. By embracing the rituals of the past, we can bring back the magic of a slower, more meaningful holiday season.

How to Incorporate Them Today

Bringing these traditions back into your life doesn't require an overhaul of your current holiday routines. Instead, you can easily adapt them for family gatherings, community events, or personal enjoyment. Whether it's organising a small carolling group, hosting a Victorian tea party, or sending handmade cards, these traditions will offer new ways to connect with the people around you.

Christmas Carolling: Door to Door or by the Fireplace

History of Carolling

Carolling dates back to medieval times when groups of singers would travel door-to-door spreading holiday cheer. The Victorian era saw a resurgence of this joyful custom, as families and friends would gather to sing together in celebration of the season. Carolling not only brought people together, but it also created a sense of community and goodwill.

Door-to-Door Carolling

There's something magical about bundling up in scarves and mittens, gathering with neighbours, and walking through the crisp winter air, singing beloved carols. Organising a carolling group is simple and rewarding. Gather a few friends or family members, choose a route through your neighbourhood, and spread some Christmas spirit.

- **Song Selection:** Stick to classic carols that evoke nostalgia, such as "Silent Night," "Deck the Halls," and "God Rest Ye Merry, Gentlemen."
- **Hot Drinks and Treats:** After the singing, offer hot chocolate, mulled cider, or homemade cookies to keep the festive spirit alive.
- **Considerations for Modern Carolling:** Be mindful of safety. Stick to well-lit areas, go in groups, and respect the privacy of others. Set a positive tone by choosing inclusive songs and ensuring everyone feels welcome.

Fireplace Carolling

If you prefer to stay indoors, hosting a carolling session around the fireplace is a cozy alternative. Invite friends or family over, light a fire, and sing together by the glow of the flames.

- **Sing-Along Ideas:** Print out lyric sheets or project them on a wall so everyone can join in.
- **Creating Atmosphere:** Dim the lights, light some candles, and add some warm blankets to set the scene for an intimate, nostalgic evening of carolling.

Victorian Christmas Tea Party

The Tradition of Victorian Tea Parties

The Victorian era was known for its elegant tea parties, especially during the holiday season. These gatherings were opportunities to celebrate friendship, share delicious food, and enjoy the warmth of good company. Recreating a Victorian tea party is a charming way to celebrate Christmas with family and friends.

How to Host Your Own Victorian Christmas Tea

- **Invitations:** Send handwritten or vintage-style invitations to evoke the spirit of a bygone era.
- **Table Setting:** Adorn your table with lace tablecloths, fine china, and silverware. Decorate with poinsettias, holly, and ivy for a festive touch.
- **Menu Ideas:**
    - **Savoury Tea Sandwiches:** Serve cucumber sandwiches, egg salad, or smoked salmon for a traditional Victorian spread.
    - **Sweet Treats:** Offer scones with clotted cream, mince pies, or a Victorian-style fruitcake.
    - **Tea Selection:** Choose loose-leaf teas like Earl Grey, Darjeeling, or herbal blends that were popular during the era.

Decor and Ambiance

Set the mood with soft classical music or Victorian carols. You can also organise parlour games, read aloud from *A Christmas Carol,* or share nostalgic stories about family Christmases of the past.

. . .

Writing and Sending Christmas Cards in the Old-Fashioned Way

History of Christmas Cards

The tradition of sending Christmas cards began in the 1840s in Victorian England. These cards were a way to send personal greetings and connect with loved ones during the holiday season.

The Tradition of Handmade Cards

In today's digital world, taking the time to create and send handmade cards can be a beautiful, personal touch. It's a simple way to show that you care and to keep alive the spirit of old-fashioned holiday cheer.

- **DIY Christmas Card Ideas:** Try your hand at stamped or watercolored designs, or incorporate pressed flowers for a rustic, natural look.
- **The Elegance of Wax Seals:** Add a vintage touch by sealing your envelopes with wax. Choose holiday motifs like snowflakes, reindeer, or a personalised family crest.

The tradition of sending Christmas cards began in the 1840s in Victorian England.

Incorporating Calligraphy

Adding calligraphy to your cards gives them a timeless, elegant feel. You don't have to be an expert—simple flowing script can add beauty to any message. Consider writing heartfelt, personal notes that reflect on the past year and your hopes for the year to come.

Combining Tradition with Modern Convenience

While handmade cards add a special touch, there's no reason to abandon digital greetings altogether. You can balance tradition with modern convenience by sending cards in both formats, ensuring your loved ones near and far receive your holiday wishes.

Additional Forgotten Traditions to Explore

- **The Yule Log:** This ancient tradition involves burning a Yule log in the hearth as a symbol of warmth and light. If you don't have a fireplace, consider lighting a smaller log-shaped candle or cake as a symbolic gesture.
- **Christmas Eve Storytelling:** Gather around the fireplace for a special night of reading classic Christmas stories, such as *Twas the Night Before Christmas* or excerpts from *A Christmas Carol*.
- **The Christmas Pickle Tradition:** Hide a pickle ornament on the Christmas tree. The first person to find it on Christmas morning receives an extra gift or treat.
- **St. Nicholas Day (December 6th):** This European tradition involves leaving shoes out for small gifts or candy. It's a fun way to celebrate the spirit of giving before Christmas Day.

CONCLUSION: Bringing Tradition into the Present

The power of traditions lies in their ability to create connections—between generations, within communities, and across time. By reviving these old-fashioned customs, you can enrich your holiday season and create moments of joy, reflection, and togetherness.

These traditions don't just bring back the past; they help us make new memories and forge a Christmas spirit that is timeless. Embrace these customs in your own way, combining them with your family's unique traditions, and discover the joy of a holiday season filled with warmth, history, and love.

Wrapping & Gifting: The Art of Handmade Presents

The Vintage Christmas Revival Guide

T he holiday season is often filled with the rush of buying presents, but there's something uniquely meaningful about a handmade gift. In times past, crafting gifts by hand was the norm—an act that required time, care, and personal touch. These presents were more than just items; they were heartfelt expressions of love and thoughtfulness.

In this chapter, we will rediscover the art of creating and wrapping homemade gifts.

By embracing the simplicity of past traditions, we can bring back the joy of giving gifts that come from the heart.

The Charm of Handmade Gifts

In a world where so many things are mass-produced, a handmade gift stands out. It tells the recipient that you've taken the time to create something just for them, something that reflects your effort, creativity, and affection. Whether it's a crocheted scarf, a jar of homemade jam, or a personalised ornament, handmade gifts carry with them a special meaning that store-bought presents can rarely match.

You don't need to be an expert crafter to make gifts by hand—many of the most cherished items are simple, yet thoughtful. This section will explore a few classic ideas for handmade presents, followed by tips on wrapping them in a way that honours the rustic charm of Christmases past.

Homemade Gift Ideas

1. Crocheted Scarves or Knitted Mittens

Nothing says cozy and personal like a handmade scarf or pair of mittens. Crocheting and knitting have been cherished crafts for centuries, offering a way to create beautiful, functional items with your own hands. Even if you're a beginner, there are plenty of easy patterns that allow you to make a thoughtful, customised gift.

- **Crocheted Scarves:** You can find simple scarf patterns that don't require advanced skills. Use soft, warm yarn in colours that you know your loved one will appreciate.
- **Knitted Mittens:** Knitted mittens are both practical and sentimental. Choose natural fibers like

wool or alpaca for warmth and durability. Consider adding a personal touch with embroidered initials or patterns that remind you of the recipient.

Nothing says cozy and personal like a handmade scarf or pair of mittens.

2. Handmade Jams or Baked Goods

Homemade jams, preserves, or baked goods are perfect gifts for friends, neighbours, or family members. These simple yet delicious presents offer a taste of your kitchen's warmth and love. You can use seasonal fruits like cranberries, apples, or oranges to create festive flavours that evoke the spirit of Christmas.

- **Jam Jars:** Use mason jars to present your jam, and add a decorative fabric cover over the lid, secured with a piece of twine.
- **Baked Goods:** Homemade cookies, gingerbread, or fruitcakes can be beautifully packaged in vintage-style tins or boxes. Add a small handwritten note or recipe card for an extra personal touch.

3. Personalized Ornaments

Another delightful handmade gift idea is creating personalized ornaments for the Christmas tree. You can make these from simple materials like felt, wood, or even dried clay. Paint or embroider names, dates, or symbols that are meaningful to the recipient. Not only will this gift brighten their tree, but it will also carry memories with it year after year.

The Art of Wrapping: Nostalgic and Rustic Presentation

Once you've crafted your homemade gifts, it's time to think about how to present them. Wrapping presents with care is an important part of the gifting experience, and it doesn't require expensive paper or ribbons. By using natural, simple materials reminiscent of past generations, you can create a charming, rustic aesthetic that reflects the heartfelt nature of your handmade gifts.

1. Brown Paper and Twine

One of the most timeless and nostalgic ways to wrap gifts is with brown kraft paper and twine. This simple, unpretentious approach has a rustic charm that feels authentic and warm. Brown paper is durable, easy to work with, and allows your creativity to shine when it comes to decorating.

- **How to Wrap:** Cut enough brown paper to cover your gift, folding the edges neatly for a clean look. Tie the package with natural jute twine, creating a simple bow at the top.
- **Personal Touches:** Add small details like hand-drawn snowflakes or stars directly onto the paper with a white pencil or chalk. You can also use a rubber stamp to print holiday motifs onto the wrapping.

2. Dried Orange Slices, Pinecones, and Greenery

Incorporating natural elements like dried orange slices, pinecones, sprigs of rosemary, or holly into your gift wrapping adds a festive, handmade feel. These materials evoke the scents and colours of the holiday season while adding texture and dimension to your presentation.

- **Dried Orange Slices:** To make dried orange slices, simply slice fresh oranges and bake them at a low temperature until they're fully dried. You can then tie them onto your gifts with twine or glue them directly onto the wrapping paper.
- **Greenery and Pinecones:** Small sprigs of evergreen or rosemary tucked under the twine provide a fresh, fragrant touch. Tiny pinecones can be hot-glued to the package for a rustic woodland feel.

3. Vintage-Inspired Gift Tags

Instead of modern store-bought gift tags, consider making your own vintage-inspired ones to enhance the nostalgic feel of your wrapping. These can be crafted using materials such as cardstock, kraft paper, or repurposed old holiday cards.

- **How to Create Vintage Tags:** Cut cardstock into simple shapes like rectangles, stars, or Christmas trees. Use a hole punch to create a space for threading twine or ribbon. Decorate the tags with hand-drawn designs, or use stamps to add holiday motifs.
- **Handwritten Notes:** Write a personalised message or the recipient's name in calligraphy or a vintage script. This small detail adds a thoughtful, elegant touch.

4. Wax Seals for an Elegant Finish

Wax seals, once used to close important letters and documents, are a beautiful way to add an elegant, old-fashioned finish to your gifts. They can be used to seal envelopes or to simply embellish the wrapping itself.

- **How to Use Wax Seals:** Melt sealing wax over the desired area, press a metal seal into the hot wax, and let it cool for a few seconds before removing. You can find wax in festive colours like red, gold, or green, and seals with holiday motifs such as snowflakes or holly.
- **Adding a Personal Touch:** You can also have a custom seal made with your family's initials or a unique symbol that holds special meaning.

COMBINING Tradition and Creativity

The beauty of handmade gifts and nostalgic wrapping lies in their authenticity. They reflect the thought, time, and love you've invested into each step of the process, from crafting the gift itself to wrapping it with care. These gifts are more than just objects; they are tokens of connection, carrying with them the spirit of the giver and the joy of the season.

Incorporating these simple yet meaningful traditions into your holiday routine doesn't just enrich your own experience—it brings a sense of warmth and personal touch to those who receive your gifts. As you make and wrap your presents, remember that the charm lies in the details: the rough edges of hand-tied twine, the scent of dried oranges, and the thoughtful notes tucked inside.

CONCLUSION: A Gift from the Heart

In a time when so much is store-bought and quickly discarded, handmade gifts and thoughtfully wrapped presents stand out as lasting, heartfelt expressions of love. By drawing on the traditions of the past—crafting scarves, baking homemade treats, and wrapping gifts with simple materials—you bring a timeless sense of care and nostalgia to your holiday celebrations.

These gifts, filled with personal meaning and creativity, will be cherished long after the holiday season ends, leaving a lasting impression on those who receive them. Embrace the joy of giving from the heart, and let the art of handmade presents add depth and warmth to your Christmas celebrations for years to come.

Playlist & Media Recommendation

The Vintage Christmas Revival Guide

As the holiday season draws near, one of the simplest yet most powerful ways to evoke nostalgia and the Christmas spirit is through music and classic holiday movies. The sounds and scenes of the holidays can transport us to cherished memories of past celebrations, filling our homes with warmth, joy, and that unmistakable festive magic.

In this chapter, we'll help you curate a vintage

Christmas playlist and offer recommendations for classic holiday movies and TV specials that can become the heart of your family traditions.

Whether you're looking for background ambiance for a quiet evening or planning a cozy family movie night, these timeless media selections will bring the nostalgic charm of Christmases past into your present celebrations.

THE MAGIC of a Vintage Christmas Playlist

No Christmas celebration feels complete without music. The melodies of old holiday classics have a way of instantly setting the mood for the season. Whether you're trimming the tree, preparing a festive dinner, or simply relaxing by the fire, a well-curated playlist featuring the voices of Bing Crosby, Frank Sinatra, and Nat King Cole will bring a timeless, comforting feel to your home.

1. BING CROSBY'S "WHITE CHRISTMAS" and Other Classics

Bing Crosby's deep, velvety voice is synonymous with Christmas. His iconic version of "White Christmas" is a must for any holiday playlist—it remains the best-selling single of all time for a reason. Crosby's holiday albums are filled with nostalgic favourites that will immediately bring you back to simpler times. A few songs to include:

- *White Christmas*
- *I'll Be Home for Christmas*
- *Silent Night*
- *Do You Hear What I Hear?*

2. Frank Sinatra's Christmas Crooning

The smooth, timeless voice of Frank Sinatra has a way of wrapping around you like a warm blanket. His Christmas recordings perfectly capture the magic of the season with a swing and style that only he could bring. Sinatra's songs often evoke the feeling of snowy nights spent indoors, surrounded by loved ones. Consider adding:

- *Have Yourself a Merry Little Christmas*
- *Jingle Bells*
- *The Christmas Waltz*
- *Let It Snow! Let It Snow! Let It Snow!*

3. Nat King Cole's Soulful Warmth

Nat King Cole's rendition of *The Christmas Song* (often known as *Chestnuts Roasting on an Open Fire*) is one of the most beloved holiday songs of all time. His voice brings a soulful warmth to every song, making you feel like you're sitting by the fire, sipping hot cocoa, and enjoying the quiet joy of the season. Must-haves include:

- *The Christmas Song (Chestnuts Roasting on an Open Fire)*
- *O Holy Night*
- *Deck the Halls*
- *Hark! The Herald Angels Sing*

4. Other Vintage Christmas Favorites

There are countless other artists from the golden age of music who contributed to the Christmas canon. Here are a few more to consider for your playlist:

- *It's Beginning to Look a Lot Like Christmas* – Perry Como
- *Rockin' Around the Christmas Tree* – Brenda Lee
- *Rudolph the Red-Nosed Reindeer* – Gene Autry
- *Jingle Bell Rock* – Bobby Helms
- *Sleigh Ride* – The Ronettes

With these songs playing in the background, your holiday gatherings will feel like stepping into a Christmas past, filled with joy and nostalgia.

As the holiday season draws near, one of the simplest yet most powerful ways to evoke nostalgia and the Christmas spirit is through music and classic holiday movies.

Classic Holiday Movies and Specials

Just like music, holiday movies and TV specials can instantly fill your home with the spirit of the season. The golden age of film brought us some of the most heartwarming and enduring Christmas movies, many of which are now staples of the holiday season. These classic films can transport us back to a simpler, more innocent time, providing the perfect backdrop for family nights by the fire.

1. "It's a Wonderful Life" (1946)

Few films capture the meaning of Christmas better than *It's a Wonderful Life*. Directed by Frank Capra and starring James Stewart, this timeless classic tells the story of George Bailey, a man who feels his life has been unremarkable until an angel shows him how much of a difference he's made in the lives of others. With themes of community, sacrifice, and gratitude, this film is a heartwarming reminder of the importance of family and friends during the holiday season.

2. "White Christmas" (1954)

This musical favourite, starring Bing Crosby and Danny Kaye, is filled with songs, dance numbers, and a lot of Christmas cheer. It follows the story of two entertainers who join forces to save a Vermont inn from closure during the holidays. The film's beautiful settings, joyful spirit, and unforgettable soundtrack (including the titular *White Christmas*) make it a perfect addition to your holiday movie lineup.

3. "Miracle on 34th Street" (1947)

Miracle on 34th Street tells the tale of a department store Santa who claims to be the real Kris Kringle and must prove his identity in court. This heartwarming film explores themes of belief, generosity, and the magic of Christmas, making it a perfect movie for families to watch together.

4. "A Christmas Carol" (1951)

Charles Dickens' classic Christmas tale has been adapted

numerous times, but this 1951 version starring Alastair Sim as Ebenezer Scrooge is one of the most beloved. The film captures the spirit of redemption, joy, and goodwill, bringing to life the timeless story of Scrooge's transformation on Christmas Eve.

5. Animated Holiday Specials from the 1960s

In the 1960s, a series of animated holiday specials became instant classics, and they remain beloved by both children and adults today. These specials are perfect for a family movie night or a quiet evening of nostalgia.

- *Rudolph the Red-Nosed Reindeer* (1964): This stop-motion animated classic tells the story of Rudolph, an outcast reindeer who finds his place guiding Santa's sleigh. Filled with charming characters and lessons about acceptance, this special has become a holiday staple.
- *A Charlie Brown Christmas* (1965): In this simple, heartfelt special, Charlie Brown searches for the true meaning of Christmas amid the commercialism of the holiday. With its gentle message and Vince Guaraldi's iconic jazz score, it's a beloved part of the holiday season.
- *How the Grinch Stole Christmas!* (1966): Based on Dr. Seuss's beloved book, this animated special features the Grinch's attempt to steal Christmas from the Whos of Whoville, only to discover that Christmas means more than just presents. Boris Karloff's narration and the timeless message make this a must-watch.

FAMILY MOVIE NIGHT: Cozy Traditions for Everyone

Holiday movie nights are a wonderful way to slow down and enjoy the season with your loved ones. There's something magical about gathering together, wrapping up in blankets, and watching a beloved Christmas film while enjoying a few seasonal treats. Here's how to turn your family movie night into a memorable holiday tradition:

1. Setting the Scene

Create a cozy atmosphere by dimming the lights and lighting a few candles. Gather up plenty of blankets and pillows so everyone can snuggle up on the couch or floor. If you have a fireplace, light it to add warmth and ambiance. You can even decorate the room with twinkle lights or set up a mini hot cocoa station nearby.

2. Movie Snacks with a Holiday Twist

No movie night is complete without snacks, and for Christmas, you can make them extra special:

- **Popcorn with a Festive Twist:** Add a holiday flair to your popcorn by mixing in melted chocolate, crushed candy canes, or cinnamon sugar.
- **Hot Cocoa Bar:** Set up a DIY hot cocoa bar with marshmallows, whipped cream, candy canes, and chocolate shavings. Let everyone create their own perfect cup.
- **Christmas Cookies:** Bake a batch of sugar cookies or gingerbread men before the movie starts, so you can enjoy fresh, warm treats as you settle in.

3. Selecting the Movie

For your family movie night, choose one of the classics mentioned earlier, depending on the mood. Want something uplifting? *It's a Wonderful Life* is perfect. Looking for something short and sweet for younger kids? Try *Rudolph the Red-Nosed Reindeer* or *A Charlie Brown Christmas*.

Conclusion: A Season of Nostalgia and Joy

Whether through timeless music, classic films, or cozy movie nights, media can transport us back to Christmases of the past, evoking memories of simpler times and the joys of the season. By curating a vintage playlist and enjoying old holiday movies with your loved ones, you'll create an atmosphere of warmth, togetherness, and nostalgia that will make your Christmas celebrations feel timeless.

So, gather your family, cue up the music, make some popcorn, and settle in for a season filled with the comforting sights and sounds of a nostalgic Christmas. These moments, shared with the people who matter most, are what make the holidays truly special.

Final Touches: Hosting a Nostalgic Christmas Party

There's something timelessly magical about hosting a Christmas party that feels steeped in nostalgia. Bringing back the charm of Christmases past, with vintage décor, classic games, and traditional dishes, can create an atmosphere of warmth and togetherness that modern gatherings sometimes miss.

In this chapter, we'll explore how to host a nostalgic-themed Christmas party, offering ideas for vintage games, a classic dinner menu, and tips for decorating your home and table with the festive spirit of yesteryear.

Creating a Nostalgic Atmosphere

The key to hosting a memorable Christmas party with a nostalgic touch is in the details. From the moment your guests walk through the door, the ambiance should transport them to a simpler time, when Christmas was about slowing down, spending time with loved ones, and celebrating the season with heartfelt traditions.

Start by setting the scene with warm lighting, soft music from the 1940s and '50s (refer to the vintage Christmas playlist in Chapter 7), and seasonal decorations that evoke the spirit of Christmases gone by. The charm of this party will lie in recreating a homey, inviting atmosphere where guests feel like they've stepped into a Christmas postcard.

Tips for Hosting a Nostalgic Christmas Party

1. Send Vintage-Style Invitations

Set the tone from the beginning by sending out vintage-inspired invitations. You could create these yourself, using cardstock and crafting materials to design old-fashioned holiday cards with handwritten notes. If you're short on time, consider purchasing vintage-style invitations featuring nostalgic Christmas images like snow-covered villages, decorated trees, or Victorian carollers.

2. Decorating with Nostalgic Flair

Your décor will play a major role in bringing the nostalgic theme to life. Start with natural elements and vintage touches to create a warm, festive ambiance.

- **Natural Decorations:** Deck your home with greenery like garlands of pine or holly, accented with

pinecones and berries. Drape them over doorways, mantels, and windows to bring the outdoors in.
- **Old-Fashioned Ornaments:** If you have a Christmas tree, decorate it with vintage-style ornaments—glass balls, wooden figures, tin icicles, and handmade decorations like strings of popcorn or cranberries.
- **Lighting:** Soft lighting is key to creating a cozy atmosphere. Use candles, fairy lights, and lanterns to give your home a warm glow reminiscent of evenings spent by the fireplace.
- **Vintage Accents:** If you have access to antique or vintage items like candlesticks, old-fashioned clocks, or retro holiday figurines, use them as part of your décor to heighten the sense of nostalgia.

3. The Playlist: Christmas Classics

Music is the heartbeat of any Christmas gathering. Refer to the vintage Christmas playlist we curated in Chapter 7, which features iconic holiday hits from Bing Crosby, Frank Sinatra, and Nat King Cole. These timeless songs will instantly transport your guests to the cozy Christmases of the past, adding warmth and charm to your gathering.

Vintage Party Games

Nostalgic party games are a wonderful way to encourage interaction and laughter among your guests. These games don't require much setup, and they're all about enjoying each other's company in a lighthearted and fun way.

1. Charades

Charades is a classic parlour game that never goes out of style. Split your guests into teams and take turns acting out holiday-themed words or phrases while the others try to guess what they are. You can keep the categories festive with options like "Christmas carols," "holiday movies," or "winter activities." It's a great way to get everyone laughing and involved.

2. Carol Sing-Along

Encourage your guests to gather around the piano (or use a playlist) for a carol sing-along. Hand out printed lyrics to traditional songs like *Silent Night, O Come, All Ye Faithful,* and *The First Noel,* and let everyone join in. If some guests are shy, keep it lighthearted and let people sing along at their own pace. For an extra touch, refer to the tips on carolling from Chapter 6, and consider offering hot drinks like mulled cider or cocoa after the sing-along.

3. Pass the Parcel

This vintage party game is great for all ages and can bring a sense of excitement and fun to your gathering. Wrap a small gift in many layers of paper. Guests sit in a circle and pass the parcel around while Christmas music plays. When the music stops, the person holding the parcel removes one layer. Continue until the final layer is unwrapped, revealing the gift for the lucky guest.

A Classic Christmas Dinner Menu

A nostalgic Christmas dinner menu focuses on comforting, traditional dishes that have been passed down through generations. The joy of these recipes lies not just in their flavours, but in the memories they evoke of past family gatherings and holiday feasts.

1. Roast Turkey or Ham

A roasted turkey or glazed ham is the centrepiece of a traditional Christmas dinner. For a nostalgic twist, use old-fashioned preparation methods, such as roasting the turkey with classic herbs like rosemary, thyme, and sage, or glazing the ham with a honey and clove mixture.

2. Side Dishes:

- **Roasted Root Vegetables:** Carrots, parsnips, and potatoes roasted with olive oil, garlic, and thyme offer a comforting and simple side dish.
- **Cranberry Sauce:** Opt for a homemade cranberry sauce with whole cranberries, orange zest, and cinnamon for a fresh, tangy addition to the meal.
- **Yorkshire Pudding or Dinner Rolls:** For a classic British touch, serve Yorkshire pudding alongside the turkey or ham. Alternatively, warm, homemade dinner rolls with butter can evoke the feeling of a family feast.

3. Desserts:

- **Christmas Pudding:** A traditional dessert filled with dried fruits, spices, and a splash of brandy, served with custard or brandy butter. The rich flavours of this old-fashioned treat make it a fitting finale for your nostalgic Christmas dinner.
- **Gingerbread Cookies:** A batch of gingerbread men adds both charm and nostalgia to your dessert table. Decorate them with icing and let your guests take part in the fun of decorating their own cookies.
- **Fruitcake:** Though sometimes maligned, a well-made fruitcake is a holiday staple for many families. Opt for a vintage recipe that balances sweetness and spice, and serve it with a cup of hot tea or coffee.

Decorating the Table with Nostalgic Elegance

The dinner table is the centrepiece of your Christmas party, and decorating it with nostalgic touches can transform the meal into a memory-filled event.

1. Homemade Centrepieces

Create a homemade centrepiece that captures the simple beauty of a traditional Christmas table. Consider using natural elements like evergreen branches, pinecones, and candles. Arrange these in a vintage bowl or along the centre of the table to create a rustic, yet elegant focal point. You can also add dried orange slices, cinnamon sticks, and cranberries for a pop of colour and festive fragrance.

2. Vintage Place Settings

To enhance the nostalgic feel, use vintage or vintage-inspired dishware. Mismatched china, delicate glassware, or antique silverware can add character and charm to the table. If you don't have access to antique pieces, opt for simple, classic white plates with cloth napkins tied with twine or ribbon for an old-world touch.

- **Place Cards:** Make handwritten place cards to set at each guest's spot. You can use vintage-style paper or even small wooden tags. Pair the cards with sprigs of rosemary or small pinecones for a natural, seasonal feel.
- **Candles and Lighting:** Candles are essential for creating a cozy, nostalgic ambiance. Arrange them in antique candleholders or place small tea lights in mason jars. Soft lighting will enhance the warmth and intimacy of the evening.

CONCLUSION: Creating Memories through Nostalgia

Hosting a nostalgic Christmas party is about more than just recreating the past—it's about slowing down, savouring traditions, and creating new memories with family and friends. By incorporating vintage games, classic holiday music, a traditional menu, and thoughtful décor, you'll transport your guests to a time when Christmas was about meaningful connections and simple joys.

As your guests gather around the table or sing carols by the fire, they'll feel the warmth of Christmases past and the love that fills the present moment. With these final touches, your party will become a lasting memory—a celebration of the holiday spirit that transcends time, bringing together the old and the new in perfect harmony.

Resource Section

I n this chapter, we offer a practical guide to help you create a nostalgic Christmas experience, no matter where you are in the world.

Whether you're looking for vintage decorations, retro cookbooks, or crafting supplies, we've compiled resources that are accessible internationally, with suggestions for both local and online options.

We've also included printable templates for ornaments, gift

tags, and paper crafts, so you can easily add homemade, nostalgic touches to your holiday celebrations.

WHERE TO FIND VINTAGE DECORATIONS, Retro Cookbooks, and Crafting Supplies

Creating a nostalgic Christmas involves gathering items that evoke the charm of Christmases past. Fortunately, there are plenty of places—both locally and online—where you can find vintage-inspired decorations, old-fashioned cookbooks, and crafting materials. The following resources are accessible from most parts of the world, giving you plenty of ways to recreate the timeless magic of a vintage holiday.

1. Thrift Stores, Flea Markets, and Local Antique Shops

In many countries, thrift stores, flea markets, and antique shops are fantastic places to search for vintage Christmas décor and retro treasures. These shops often carry a wide variety of items, including nostalgic holiday ornaments, old-fashioned dishware, and traditional Christmas décor that can help you set the perfect scene for your celebrations.

- **Local Thrift Stores and Charity Shops:** Depending on your location, secondhand stores such as Oxfam (UK), Emmaus (France), or Humana (Spain and other European countries) offer affordable vintage decorations. Regularly browse these stores, as their stock changes frequently.
- **Flea Markets:** Flea markets are popular worldwide and can be found in many cities and towns. From vintage tree ornaments to antique candle holders, you

can often find unique, nostalgic Christmas items. Look for handmade decorations or traditional holiday crafts native to your region.
- **Antique Shops:** Local antique shops can be treasure troves for holiday items that date back decades. Search for vintage Christmas baubles, retro lights, and holiday figurines, which are often available worldwide.

2. Online Marketplaces and Shops

For those who prefer the convenience of shopping from home, there are many online options that cater to international customers and specialise in vintage and nostalgic Christmas items. These platforms allow you to search for specific items and ship them to most destinations around the world.

- **Etsy (Global):** Etsy is an international platform where sellers from around the world offer vintage Christmas décor, retro crafting supplies, and handmade holiday items. You'll find everything from mid-century glass ornaments to vintage wrapping paper and retro-inspired holiday decorations.
- **eBay (Global):** eBay has a vast selection of vintage holiday items, including Christmas ornaments, classic tree toppers, and retro holiday dinnerware. Since sellers are located globally, it's easy to find items that can be shipped to your location.
- **Trove Market (US & International):** Trove is an online marketplace that features vintage and antique home décor, including holiday items. Many sellers ship internationally, making it a great resource for finding unique, nostalgic Christmas decorations.

3. Craft Stores for Handmade Touches

If you're planning to create your own nostalgic Christmas decorations or gifts, craft stores and suppliers are essential. Many countries have well-known chains and local shops that carry everything you need for a DIY vintage Christmas, and many online retailers ship internationally.

- **Michaels (North America, Shipping Worldwide):** Michaels is a large craft store offering a wide range of crafting materials, including holiday-themed supplies like vintage-style ribbons, crafting paper, and materials for making homemade ornaments or wreaths.
- **Joann Fabrics (US, International Shipping):** Joann Fabrics specialises in fabrics and supplies for sewing and crafting. It's a great place to find materials for creating vintage-inspired table runners, stockings, or handmade gifts.
- **Hobbycraft (UK, Shipping Internationally):** Hobbycraft offers a wide variety of crafting materials and holiday décor supplies. You'll find everything from paper crafting materials to vintage-inspired stamps and paints.

4. Retro Cookbooks and Recipe Inspiration

Recreating a traditional holiday meal often requires looking back to classic recipes. Retro cookbooks, whether found in local bookshops or online, are a wonderful resource for traditional Christmas dishes. Many of these books offer recipes from past eras, allowing you to bring authentic flavours to your nostalgic Christmas feast.

- **Local Used Bookstores:** Many countries have secondhand bookshops where you can find retro cookbooks and classic Christmas recipes. In Europe, stores like Shakespeare and Company in Paris or Foyles in London often stock old-fashioned cookbooks with holiday menus.
- **Online Marketplaces (Etsy, eBay):** Both Etsy and eBay feature vintage cookbooks from around the world, often focused on holiday recipes. Search for cookbooks from specific decades or regions to find traditional Christmas dishes that suit your nostalgic menu.
- **National Libraries or Book Exchanges:** Many national libraries have collections of old cookbooks that can be accessed online. Additionally, book exchanges or community library programs (such as Little Free Libraries) often feature classic cookbooks that have been passed down through generations.

Printable Templates for Ornaments, Gift Tags, and Paper Crafts

Bringing a personal, handmade touch to your Christmas decorations is easier than ever with printable templates. Whether you're creating nostalgic ornaments for the tree, adding vintage-style gift tags to presents, or making classic paper crafts, these printable designs can be easily downloaded and customised to your liking.

1. Printable Ornament Templates

Making homemade ornaments can be a fun, family-friendly activity, and these printable templates allow you to craft vintage-style ornaments with minimal materials.

- **Paper Snowflakes:** Use our snowflake templates to create intricate, vintage-style paper snowflakes. Print them on white paper, or try using pastel colours or old book pages for a nostalgic twist. You can hang them from your tree or use them as window decorations.
- **3D Paper Stars:** These 3D star templates are easy to fold and assemble, adding depth and charm to your Christmas tree or garlands. Print on cardstock, cut, and fold along the lines to create a classic Christmas decoration.
- **Paper Angels:** Simple but beautiful, these printable paper angel templates can be used as ornaments, garlands, or even table decorations. Print them on cardstock, and let your guests or family members decorate them with glitter or paint.

2. Printable Gift Tag Templates

Gift tags are a small but significant detail in any nostalgic Christmas celebration. With these printable templates, you can create your own vintage-inspired tags to attach to presents, making your gifts feel personal and unique.

- **Classic Holiday Motifs:** These gift tags feature timeless Christmas images like holly, Christmas trees, and snowflakes. Print them on cardstock or kraft paper and tie them onto gifts with twine or ribbon for a rustic, old-fashioned look.
- **Vintage Typography:** Inspired by retro design, these gift tags feature holiday greetings in classic fonts. Perfect for adding a touch of elegance, these tags can be printed on cream or white paper and embellished with wax seals (see Chapter 8 for tips).

- **Customisable Tags:** Our customisable gift tag templates leave space for you to add names, personal messages, or drawings. Print these templates in black and white, and encourage children or family members to colour them in, adding a personal, homemade touch to every gift.

3. Printable Paper Craft Templates

Paper crafts were a popular way to create holiday decorations in past generations, and these printable templates allow you to bring that tradition into your home. These simple, nostalgic crafts are ideal for families or anyone who loves making things by hand.

- **DIY Paper Garlands:** Use these printable shapes—stars, hearts, bells, or Christmas trees—to create your own paper garlands. String them together with thread or ribbon and drape them across the tree, mantel, or around the house for a classic holiday look.
- **Pop-up Christmas Cards:** These printable pop-up card templates offer a fun twist on the classic Christmas card. Featuring festive images like Christmas trees or reindeer, they can be printed on cardstock and assembled easily for a personal, interactive holiday greeting.
- **Advent Calendar:** Our printable vintage-style Advent calendar template is a delightful way to count down to Christmas. Behind each numbered window, you can place small treats, festive messages, or family activity suggestions for each day leading up to Christmas.

ADDITIONAL INTERNATIONAL CRAFTING and DIY Inspiration

Here are some globally accessible resources for finding inspiration and crafting ideas for your nostalgic Christmas celebration:

1. Pinterest (Global)

Pinterest is an international platform offering endless inspiration for vintage holiday crafts, décor, and gift ideas. Search for terms like "vintage Christmas crafts," "DIY nostalgic Christmas," or "retro holiday décor" to find projects suitable for your skill level and region.

2. YouTube Crafting Channels (Global)

YouTube is home to countless crafting channels that provide tutorials on how to create your own nostalgic Christmas decorations and gifts. Channels like "Crafts and DIY" or "Hometalk" offer tutorials accessible worldwide, helping you create everything from handmade ornaments to vintage-inspired wreaths.

3. Crafting Blogs (Global)

Several international crafting blogs specialise in DIY holiday projects and vintage-inspired décor. Many of these blogs provide printable templates, tutorials, and step-by-step guides.

- **The Graphics Fairy:** A great resource for vintage clip art and free printables, ideal for crafting nostalgic holiday decorations.
- **Craftberry Bush:** This blog offers seasonal craft ideas, including Christmas projects with a nostalgic or rustic touch, accessible from anywhere in the world.
- **Vintage Revivals:** Specialises in upcycling and crafting vintage-inspired décor with easy-to-follow instructions, perfect for your nostalgic Christmas projects.

Afterword: The Timeless Magic of Christmas

Afterword: The Timeless Magic of Christmas

As the holiday season unfolds each year, we are reminded of the beauty and power of tradition. Christmas is a time to pause, to reflect, and to gather with the ones we hold dear, creating moments that will linger in our hearts for years to come. The traditions, recipes, and nostalgic ideas shared in this book are just a glimpse into the rich tapestry of ways Christmas has been celebrated across different eras and cultures.

By embracing the simpler, more meaningful aspects of the holiday—whether through handmade gifts, time-honoured games, or a festive gathering that brings the spirit of the past into the present—we not only honour those who came before us but also create lasting memories for future generations. As you incorporate

Afterword: The Timeless Magic of Christmas

these traditions into your own holiday celebrations, remember that each Christmas is an opportunity to blend the old with the new, to weave together history and modern life into something uniquely your own.

But as we say goodbye to this chapter of rediscovering nostalgic holiday magic, the story doesn't end here. Christmas is ever-evolving, and its traditions adapt, year after year, across the world. There are still countless stories untold, traditions yet to be rediscovered, and new ways to celebrate the season.

What about the forgotten customs of other holidays? What hidden gems remain tucked away in the corners of history, waiting to be unearthed for Easter, Halloween, or even summer solstice celebrations?

Perhaps the next chapter lies not in what we already know—but in the traditions we have yet to explore.

The story continues...

www.ingramcontent.com/pod-product-compliance
Lightning Source LLC
Chambersburg PA
CBHW051725261125
35889CB00026B/1365